THE STYLE OF TIME

© 2022 ACC Art Books
World copyright reserved

ISBN: 9781788841955

First published in Italian under the title Lo Stile del Tempo in 2022 by White Star

WS White Star Publishers® is a registered trademark property of White Star s.r.l.
© 2022 White Star s.r.l.
Piazzale Luigi Cadorna, 6
20123 Milan, Italy
www.whitestar.it

This translation published by in 2022 ACC Art Books by agreement with White Star s.r.l.

The right of Mara Cappelletti to be identified as author of this work has been asserted by her in accordance with the Copyright, Designs and Patents Act 1988

All rights reserved. No part of this publication may be reproduced, stored in a retrieval system, or transmitted in any form or by any means electronic, mechanical, photocopying, recording or otherwise, without the prior permission of the publisher.

The author and publisher gratefully acknowledge the permission granted to reproduce the copyright material in this book. Every effort has been made to trace copyright holders and to obtain their permission for the use of copyright material. Any errors or omissions are entirely unintentional and should be addressed to the publisher.

British Library Cataloguing-in-Publication Data
A catalogue record for this book is available from the British Library

English Edition
Translator: Megan Bredeson
Editors: Phillip Gaskill, White Star; Sue Bennett, ACC Art Books
Production: Steve Farrow, ACC Art Books

Printed in Slovenia
for ACC Art Books Ltd, Woodbridge, Suffolk, IP12 4SD, UK
www.accartbooks.com

MARA CAPPELLETTI

THE STYLE OF TIME

THE EVOLUTION OF WRISTWATCH DESIGN

ACC ART BOOKS

Contents

THE STYLE OF TIME 7

THE EARLY 1900s 19

THE 1910s 35

THE 1920s 53

THE 1930s 75

THE 1940s 99

THE 1950s 121

THE 1960s 155

THE 1970s 175

THE 1980s 195

THE 1990s 211

THE 2000s 243

THE STYLE OF TIME

Time is a great mystery: a mutable, expanding or disappearing principle belonging to an uncertain dimension – one that, more than any other, depends on the perception of one's mind. Yet it also appears concrete, marked by the passing of hours, days, and years. Probing this mystery has presented a significant challenge to humankind, who, over the centuries, has felt the need to assign specific deadlines to anything in continuous flow. The path towards capturing the minutes and seconds has coincided with phases of scientific evolution, allowing for the manufacture of increasingly reliable timepieces that were also attuned to changes in custom and aesthetic canons.

A watch is a work of technical mastery. It also constitutes an artifact that blends art with science, creating what over the years has become, and remained, an object of desire.

In fine and applied arts, "style" defines the combination of formal traits that make an object distinctive, tracing it back to a specific era, or even to the person who first introduced them.

Certainly, a watch can also be viewed as a product whose stylistic code is linked to the aesthetics of a particular era, and judgment upon its taste must be read through the frameworks that belong to that era.

Consider, for example, the timepieces that emerged during the 1920s, conveying the linearity of Art Deco through their rectangular cases. In order to adapt to the tastes at the time, which preferred straight lines, the traditional circular structure of the watch underwent a significant change. Up to that point, the circle had constituted, with few exceptions, the "shape" of horology, and even mechanical movements were adapted to it. The restraint of the Bauhaus style would influence the essential aesthetics of 1930s and 1940s timepieces; and during the 1980s, the fun, colourful design of the Memphis Group spread, and Swatches and suchlike were born.

In some cases, it was a model's individual story which influenced its shape and style. Consider the Tank, conceived in 1917 by Louis Cartier, which has the shape of a military tank, specifically the Renault FT-17 used during the First World War. In other cases, it is from necessity related to use, as with Reverso, designed by Jaeger-LeCoultre in 1931. Its "flappable" case was a technical solution made at the request of polo players, but it also became a history-making aesthetic solution.

These specimens are created within a highly specific context, on which their shape and structure depend. From this perspective, the production of watches might be seen as closely tied to culture and society. This is confirmed in the thesis of Heinrich Wölfflin, a Swiss art historian of the early twentieth century who declared that style is the expression of an era.

To illustrate the phenomenon of watchmaking, it is advisable to take into account the aspects concerning the "context" in which a certain model was created – that is, the nature of its presence in society and its relationship with social dynamics. Both the First and Second World Wars spurred the production of reliable timepieces with special features for reading the dial and checking the time. The chronometers and chronographs that spread beginning in the 1930s responded to the need for ever more precisely determine timings during car races, transatlantic flights, and the Olympic games; offerings by Eberhard, Longines, Omega, Patek Philippe and Rolex, among others, would satisfy these needs. At times it was difficult to establish whether the needs of a given era stimulated its technical solutions, or whether mechanical innovation was what led to the development of new styles; but both views are true.

When considering the watch as an expression of applied art and describing it through various disciplines, we must not overlook the practical and utilitarian element constituting its chief function: keeping time. In the past, the applied arts have often been considered minor, as they are linked to "manufacturing", intended for the body, as opposed to the "creating" of the superior fine arts, intended for the soul and intellect.

In the case of watchmaking, however, the element of knowledge and invention overcomes the contrast between science and art. The ability to mark

Gold bracelet watch with diamonds and enamel, made in 1868 by Patek Philippe, then sold to the Hungarian Countess Koscowicz. It is a model specifically designed to be worn on the wrist, rather than an altered pocket or pendant timepiece.

— THE STYLE OF TIME

A set of historical watches by IWC Schaffhausen.

time is closely linked to a technical evolution that is an art in itself, one that has evolved over the centuries, reaching refined degrees of perfection.

Certainly, the introduction of the waterproof case and an automatic movement by Rolex in the late 1920s and early 1930s changed the story of watchmaking forever, setting the standard for sports watches.

The "style" accords with the characteristic aspects of an era and a tradition, as well as the production. "Style" also denotes the system of formal and expressive means distinguishing the way in which designers, and, in the case of this book, watchmaking firms, express themselves. Case shapes, the graphic design of dials, the selection of hands, formal details – each manufacturer is well identified by a series of components.

In the past, watches were, and still are, laden with values pertaining to personal identity and power. Only a limited number of people could afford to buy wristwatches at the beginning of the last century: this was a small, elite group of people who, using this instrument, could exercise control over their "personal" time. Some watches' stories are linked to those of their owners, be they aviators, pilots, explorers or collectors.

Finally, "style" also constitutes a habitual mode of behaviour, action and speech. It links with the concept of costume and, ultimately, of fashion. Watches are not only symbols of wealth and taste, but also tools with the ability to reflect and communicate the personal character and temperament of their wearers.

Conquering Time

How often in a day do we rotate our wrists slightly to glance at our watches? Countless times, without our even realising it. The gesture is simple, yet extremely significant. By controlling the time, we put our lives in order. We avoid missing professional appointments, or meetings with friends. This is obvious to us, but it has not always been this way. Throughout history, possession of a way to measure time has been the privilege of a few.

The sources relating the birth of the first wristwatch are multiple, and not always in agreement. According to Martin Huber and Alan Banbery, authors of historical publications on Patek Philippe, the oldest model of wristwatch is cited in connection with Robert Dudley, Earl of Leicester, master horseman and favourite of Queen Elizabeth I: it is said that in

1571, he offered the queen a small watch that was fastened to her wrist with a bracelet. In the seventeenth century, reference is made to a watch that philosopher and mathematician Blaise Pascal wore on his wrist: it was completely unusual at the time, especially in an era when men did not adorn their arms.

Accounts also tell of a wedding gift offered in 1805 by Empress Joséphine Bonaparte to her daughter-in-law Amalia Augusta, daughter of King Maximilian of Bavaria. In 1868, the Patek Philippe workshops created for the Countess Koscowicz of Hungary a wristwatch in gold, diamonds and black enamel. This is one of the first women's watch-

In 2008, Omega introduced the Si14 balance spring, named for the chemical symbol and atomic number of silicon. Thanks to silicon's non-magnetic properties, the functioning of the Si14 balance spring is not compromised by exposure to magnetic objects. This means that timepieces fitted with the Si14 balance spring perform significantly higher in precision tests compared to those with mechanisms from traditional materials.

es about which there is historical certainty. However, the above are unique specimens.

One must arrive at the beginning of the twentieth century for models to emerge that would herald the new way in which watches were worn – on the wrist. Nearly all the earliest known wristwatches – and various watchmakers vie for the distinction of having made the first ones – were made for women. Gentlemen preferred to wear watches in their waistcoat pockets. These were much more sizeable, but also more robust and reliable.

The first watches conceived and designed for the male public, produced according to precise technical objectives in a plurality of identical specimens, were made in 1880 by Girard-Perregaux for the officers of the German Navy. However, this manufacture was still limited, and the models were highly technical. The watch would also need to develop an aesthetic before it would spread.

A strong impetus for the development of wristwatches came from the need to tell the time quickly and easily during flight experiments, first by civilians and later by those in the military field. Time is a key factor in defining movement in space and in aviation, and knowing your exact position can make the difference between life and death.

Initially, pilots simply adapted pocket watches by tying them to leather straps and fastening them to their arm or leg so they could see the time during flight. Then came the Santos de Cartier, designed in 1904 by Louis Cartier for the Brazilian adventurer and aviator Alberto Santos-Dumont, who connected the wristwatch with fashion and style. What followed was an explosion in the development of designs; a continuous technical evolution; and a product in constant growth over the decades to follow.

The infinite range of technical and aesthetic solutions would satisfy the needs of scientific exploration and also of style, up until the quartz crisis of the 1970s. The traditional watchmaking market appeared to be in serious trouble at the time – finished, according to some; instead, yet another transformation was taking place. Several factors contributed to the revival of the sector.

The Swiss industry worked to improve mechanical timepieces while making them less expensive to produce. It did so by improving production through the use of faster machines with higher levels of control, but also by applying standardisation criteria to processes and components.

▼ Following pages:
Panerai Luminor watch featuring a crown-protecting bridge, a distinctive feature of this model.

At the same time, however, historical high-end companies that could count on the strength of their brands responded by altering their marketing and communication strategies, turning their watches into status symbols, indicating not only quality but also style – meaning, in this case, a lifestyle.

In *The Theory of the Leisure Class*, American economist Thorstein Veblen argued that when companies confer prestige and project a reputation for quality, a high price can stimulate demand rather than knock it down, since these brands serve as emblems of exclusivity.

Patek Philippe launched an advertisement that announced "A Patek Philippe doesn't just tell you the time. It tells you something about yourself"; Vacheron Constantin compared their watches to "rare works of art"; Audemars Piguet presented them as an "exclusive creation for the

Perpetual calendar edition of the Royal Oak by Audemars Piguet. Pink gold case and bracelet. Silver-toned dial with "Grande Tapisserie" pattern, pink gold applied hour indices and Royal Oak hands with luminescent coating, silver-toned inner bezel.

discerning few"; and Piaget, in the same period, introduced their timepiece as "the most expensive watch in the world."[1]

The 1970s were also the decade when watchmaking houses relied on design. It was a designer, Gérald Genta, who created some of the most successful watch models, including the Nautilus and the Royal Oak, presenting steel watches as luxury items.

This brings us to the 1980s, when wristwatch-making had a new technical and creative impetus. In that decade, a market developed for collecting vintage watches, and has since been rapidly expanding, leading Swiss workshops to introduce new models inspired by historical and iconic models of the past. The 1990s saw the return of complications, including grand complications.

The history of watches is closely linked with the history of costume and design, but some watch models have become cult objects, transcending their own eras.

These models are coveted objects in modern times. A mechanical watch embodies the magic of a technical knowledge that still fascinates; it holds intrinsic, intangible values, linked to the prestige of owning an object sought after for its design and mechanics. The question is not just one of luxury as a status symbol, but also of the pursuit of creative and cultural excellence.

Since the early twentieth century, the wristwatch has accompanied, and will continue to accompany, people in their lives, in many cases becoming the protagonist of fascinating stories. This volume outlines the evolution of wristwatch-making through the decades of the twentieth century, using select models to illustrate changes in shape and style, as well as the costume, historical and artistic contexts in which they were conceived.

---

[1] LANDES, DAVID S., Revolution in Time: Clocks and the Making of the Modern World, Belknap Press, Harvard University Press, Cambridge, MA, 1984.

The Early 1900s

The Belle Époque

The historical period now called the "Belle Époque" was characterised by optimism, faith in progress, and *joie de vivre*. The period from the last decades of the nineteenth century up to the outbreak of the First World War was marked by political peace and widespread economic wellbeing. The world, or at least a portion of it, was savouring the euphoria of festivities that seemingly had no end. Instead, they would be tragically interrupted with the beginning of conflict in 1914. In this context of peace and economic growth, invention and advances in technology and science were, compared to past epochs, unparalleled. The incandescent light bulb patented by Thomas Edison in 1880 allowed for the spread of public electric lighting in cities. Studies by Guglielmo Marconi led to the invention of the radio; Alexander Graham Bell forever changed communication by patenting the telephone; and Louis and Auguste Lumière astounded audiences with their first film screenings.

The transport sector had expanded enormously; by 1913, the railway network had reached one million kilometres (620,000 miles), and the first cars sped along the streets, to the amazement of passers-by. Maritime transport also experienced extensive development, with the construction of transatlantic liners able to accommodate travellers in comfort and luxury; on these cruise ships, time was spent among dances, tennis matches, gala dinners, and various forms of entertainment. Between the end of the nineteenth century and the beginning of the twentieth, technological discoveries, welcomed with great enthusiasm, also inspired the world of art, becoming the subject of the ballet *Excelsior*, conceived by Italian choreographer Luigi Manzotti and set to music by the composer Romualdo Marenco. It celebrated the triumph of science through eight scenes in which the allegorical figures of Light and of Civilisation battle Obscurantism on the stage.

◀ *Gilbert Parker, Canadian-born author and British politician, shown c. 1905.*

— THE EARLY 1900s

"Illumination of the Main Entrance to the Paris Exhibition", from a watercolour by Tony Grubhofer, 1900.

THE EARLY 1900s

The universal expositions and world's fairs held irregularly in various cities in Europe (London, Paris, Barcelona, Milan, Turin) and the United States (St. Louis, San Francisco) were the perfect context for showcasing innovations in technology, science and art to the general public.

The *Exposition Universelle* held in Paris in 1900, whose theme was *"le bilan d'un siècle"* ("the assessment of a century"), attracted thousands of people to the French capital looking to admire the works of art, the decorative style of Art Nouveau in both architecture and the applied arts, and, of course, the marvels of the Eiffel Tower, inaugurated one year earlier.

In this context of widespread comfort, political security, trust in progress, and industrial and commercial development, the upper middle class faced life with exuberance and panache, convinced that they were living in a happy, carefree era that would endure forever.

A Style Attentive to Details

The worldly opportunities offered by city life were innumerable, and every occasion required the appropriate dress: ceremonial or ball gowns were worn for important festivities, as well as for going to the theatre, opera, ballet, and even the cabaret.

At the beginning of the twentieth century, the clothing sector could rely on a giant market extending throughout Europe and the United States. The most significant centre of production was certainly Paris, where fashion ateliers and the most renowned jewellers resided on rue de la Paix and place Vendôme.

If ladies frequented the ateliers of Charles Worth or Paul Poiret to have the most elegant

A pocket watch by Girard-Perregaux, La Esmeralda Tourbillon, was awarded a gold medal at the 1889 Paris Universal Exhibition.

— THE EARLY 1900s

The first successful flight of the Wright Flyer*. Orville Wright is at the aircraft controls, lying prone on the lower wing as he operates its wing-warping mechanism. Meanwhile, Wilbur Wright is at the side to provide balance for the machine and has just let go of the right-hand wing.*

and refined dresses made, their spouses instead went to London, especially to Savile Row, a street in the city centre where tailoring workshops were based which specialised in men's fashion.

In the latter decades of the nineteenth century, the most formal garment for men was the frock coat during the day and a formal tailcoat in the evening. With the beginning of the new century, the three-piece suit began to take over in daytime; it consisted of a jacket, waistcoat and trousers, never in colours that were too bold, and worn with shirts with starched high collars and rigid shirtfronts. Eveningwear continued to be highly formal: foremost of these was "white tie" or "full evening" dress with a tailed dress coat, though "black tie" or "dinner jacket" dress, also known as the tuxedo,[1] considered more informal, was gaining acceptance.

The tie offered a single note of colour and could soften the sober rigour of men's clothing. At times it was secured with a pin, which was useful in keeping the knot fixed: this ornament often

---

[1] The tuxedo consisted of a black jacket with its distinctive silk lapels and matching trousers, often worn with a starched white shirt, a shirtfront, and a cummerbund – which could be either black to match the suit or white to match the shirt. A bow tie, on the other hand, was co-ordinated with one's waistcoat (vest); white ties and vests were customary on the most elegant occasions.

matched the wearer's collar buttons and cufflinks. A standout among men's accessories was the pocket watch, placed inside the waistcoat pocket and fastened with a chain. With a circular shape, it usually featured a lid to protect its dial, decorated with a monogram, crest or unique engravings. The lid itself could be worked to feature the complex, sinuous shapes typical of Art Nouveau.

Experiments in Flight

In the early twentieth century, science appeared to make anything possible; even one of the most ancient and unattainable dreams of man, flight, was no longer a mere illusion. Thanks to technological progress in the field of materials and the development of engines, various people had dedicated themselves to research in the field of aeronautics, both in Europe and in the United States.

In America, brothers Wilbur and Orville Wright worked on a motorised aircraft, constructing both its engine and its propellers. On 17 December 1903, after many unsuccessful attempts, Wilbur managed to keep the aircraft, dubbed the *Flyer,* in the air for fifty-nine seconds, covering a distance of 260 metres (852 feet).

For a more convenient way for an aircraft's pilot to check the time than on a dial, the two brothers turned to Vacheron Constantin, who created a watch with chronometer. It was fitted with a long leather strap, to be fixed around the thigh so that reading it was comfortable once the pilot was sitting at the aircraft controls. This was a unique piece which was not mass-produced.

In Paris, on 12 November 1906, the Franco-Brazilian aviation pioneer Alberto Santos-Dumont flew the *14-bis* plane. Santos-Dumont had realised his dream of flying, which was born during his childhood while living in Brazil. Reading the fantastical adventures of Jules Verne, he had begun to build aeroplanes using rubber bands and tiny balloons. Santos designed and piloted fourteen hydrogen-inflated airships with a gasoline-powered propulsion engine. The last of these were fitted with wings and gas tanks, to the point that No. 14, equipped with ailerons for flight control and with landing gear, now had the structure of a plane and was named *14-bis*.

The rich and extravagant heir Alberto Santos-Dumont became an icon in early-twentieth-century Paris. The fact that tables in his home were placed at a height of 2 metres (6½ feet), and that to reach the chairs one had to use a ladder or footstool, certainly contributed to his fame. His idea was to make everyone feel the thrill of being raised off the ground. But the element that defined him more than any other in terms of style was that he inspired the birth of the first men's wristwatch: the Santos, which jeweller-artist Louis Cartier created especially for the daring aviator.

Gilberte Gautier, author of *Cartier: The Legend*,[2] writes that the friendship between these two men was born on an evening organised by Baron Deutsch de la Meurthe in 1900, one of the many social occasions in which societal elite participated. The following year, the Brazilian confided to Louis Cartier that his pocket watch did not allow him to easily check timing and performance while commanding his airship. Cartier designed and built a slim timepiece for Santos-Dumont to be tied to his wrist with

---

[2]   Gilberte, Gautier, *Cartier: The Legend*, Arlington Books, London, 1983.

a leather strap and closed with a small clasp.

Flying Machines and Time Machines

A pre-eminent presence on the French luxury market, Cartier had defined and popularised the "garland style" in jewellery during the Belle Époque period. The company was, however, always ready to integrate innovative solutions, on both aesthetic and functional levels. In 1898, at the age of 23, young Louis, the most creative and innovative mind in the family, became his father Alfred's business partner and married Andrée-Caroline Worth. This established an artistic and commercial partnership between the jewellery firm and the fashion house Worth, which led Cartier to brilliant success. The *maison* counted the richest dynasties in the world among its clients, and this clientele was always ready for new creations. Louis decided to include pocket watches, clocks and wristwatches among its novelties. As for the pocket watch, the model that still sold the largest number of pieces, Cartier obtained supplies from the best Swiss watchmakers of the time, such as Audemars Piguet and Vacheron Constantin.[3]

The major goal of Cartier making watches in-house would become a reality by virtue of a meeting between the firm's representative and one of the most creative minds in watchmaking, Edmond Jaeger.

Thanks to the genius of Jaeger, a passionate inventor of ultra-thin movements, the watch that Santos-Dumont had asked of Cartier was born. Since the prototype of the Santos watch, made as a one-off, does not appear in the house's logs, its exact "date of birth" cannot be determined. However, the advertisement accompanying the launch of the automatic Santos in 1978 says "If you want to wear the watch worn by people at the top since 1904[,] wear a Cartier." This would seem to endorse the commonly accepted date, 1904, as that of its invention.

It is from this custom-made example that the first wristwatch, not for military use but still aimed at a male audience, would be born. Cartier was innovative not only in terms of creation, but also in terms of communication: characteristic of this model was that it would actually be introduced on the market with a name, that of the aviator to whom the first watch was dedicated, and therefore be very easily identifiable. The first Santos that went on sale to the public in the rue de la Paix was duly recorded in their 1911 books. The entry *"Montre de forme carré dite Santos-Dumont"* ("Square-shaped watch, called Santos-Dumont") instead refers to a ten-line platinum watch, also with a movement signed by Jaeger, which was sold to Count Kinsky on 30 January 1913.[4]

Aerial Explorations

Only a few years after the first strenuous attempts to lift an aircraft into the air, aviation technology had become refined enormously, and aircraft flew across the skies, achieving new records.

---

[3] Osvaldo Patrizzi, Cartier Bianco, Patrizzi & Co. Editions, Milan, 2011, p. 9.
[4] Jader Barracca - Giampiero Negretti - Franco Nencini, Le temps de Cartier, Wrist International, Milan, 1989, p. 46.

Alberto Santos-Dumont aboard his plane, called the 14-bis. Portrait taken by Paul Tissandier, 1906.

— THE EARLY 1900s

In July 1909, in Calais, aviation pioneer Louis Blériot was aboard his monoplane, the Blériot XI. That night the wind had dropped, and it appeared that the right moment had come to accept a challenge launched by the British newspaper the *Daily Mail*: to cross the English Channel onboard a flying machine. Some thought it a fantasy, but Blériot managed to accomplish the feat in thirty-seven minutes. Among his navigational tools was a Zenith watch. "I am very satisfied with my Zenith watch, which I regularly wear. I can only recommend it to anyone who is accustomed to accuracy," the aviator said of his timepiece. It was equipped with a black dial with contrasting luminescent hands and numbers, to guarantee optimal legibility in all light conditions. It was a prototype from which watches for pilots would be developed.

From Pocket Watches to Wristwatches

Wristwatches were actually used as early as the latter nineteenth century, albeit only in the military sphere. By 1880, Girard-Perregaux had created a series of two thousand wristwatches for William I of Prussia's Imperial naval officers, but it was a special production and made no contribution to the wider spread of such a model. We might instead consider these the forefathers of military watchmaking.

From the earliest history of wristwatch-making, therefore, two distinct types of watches were already emerging: those that played with the many variations of the model's different styles and designs, and those that experimented with their equally varied technical formation.

Eberhard & Co., designed in 1905. *A watch indicating the hours and minutes by means of two rotating discs, with a telemetric scale and a tachymeter scale to one fifth of a second. Hand-wound mechanical movement. This unique timepiece received two patents in 1905.*

In 1905, it was Eberhard & Co. who introduced a novelty in wristwatch-making, a chronograph with a single-button timer, a special device for reading the hours and minutes which was viewable through an open window on the dial.

Complications – i.e., all additional information enriching the functional value of the timepiece beyond the simple reading of the time on the dial – had existed for centuries in

Audemars Piguet, Minute Repeater Watch. *Audemars Piguet made its first minute repeater wristwatch in 1892. The watch was produced by the Le Brassus manufacture and delivered to watchmaker Louis Brandt et Frère in Bienne, Switzerland. The Bienne company would later take the name of Omega.*

pocketwatch-making. In these times of great technical development, however, the challenge was to further miniaturise watches' mechanical components, so that wristwatches could also be "complicated". In 1892, Audemars Piguet created a model with a minute repeater complication,[5] and acquired a reputation as a manufacturer of complicated small-diameter wristwatches, which the manufacturer would begin to produce and market successfully from 1905.

Although these were limited productions, they were characterised by a great variety of aesthetic variations, which would be further expanded in the years to follow. François Chaille, a scholar of the Audemars Piguet firm, comments that beginning in 1911, the *maison* also offered women's models with minute repeaters (including the only one in existence with a central seconds hand) mounted on jewelled watches set in diamonds. The audacity of such a creation is still evident today, a century later, given that the complicated women's watch appears to be too daring a subject.[6]

Patek Philippe made a women's watch with a minute repeater complication in 1916.

The ladies showed off smaller, beautifully decorated timepieces crafted from precious metals and bedazzled with precious stones.

At the same time, some watchmakers worked hard to develop wrist chronographs.

Although the era of the wristwatch had been inaugurated, the era of the pocket watch was not yet over. The latter, in fact, continued to prevail over the former for a considerable length of time.

---

[5] The minute repeater is a mechanical watch complication that indicates the time by means of acoustics.

[6] François Chaille, Audemars Piguet: Master Watchmaker Since 1875, Rizzoli International Publications with Éditions Flammarion, 2011.

— THE EARLY 1900s

Pocket watch in gold and enamel
René Lalique   circa 1900

Lalique was responsible for the decoration of select watch models, displaying his mastery of metal and enamel work in yet another field. This hunting watch is finely crafted in gold and has a quarter repeater complication. The decorative style can clearly be attributed to Art Nouveau, wherein inspiration from the natural world prevails. The typical trumpet-shaped bignonias, at times referred to as the "Trompette de Jéricho", stand out in their bright yellow and orange tones.

    The rhinoceros beetle seems to have been a favourite of René Lalique's and recurs as a decorative element throughout his work.

    A symbolic reading of the decorations shows the meaning behind the "trumpet of Jericho", one of spiritual weaponry prevailing over earthly struggles, while the scarab represents personal renewal, positive change, and prosperity.

    A similarly decorated watch by Lalique, with the same flowers and a rhinoceros beetle, but with a movement by Patek Philippe (# 97537), is in the Patek Philippe Museum. Another watch decorated by Lalique, depicting bats and butterflies, was auctioned at Sotheby's on 16 February 2013 for US$930,837 (approx. £651,586) then setting the world record for a Lalique watch sold at auction.

René Lalique, Pocket watch in gold and enamel, c. 1900.

THE EARLY 1900s —

~1900

— THE EARLY 1900s

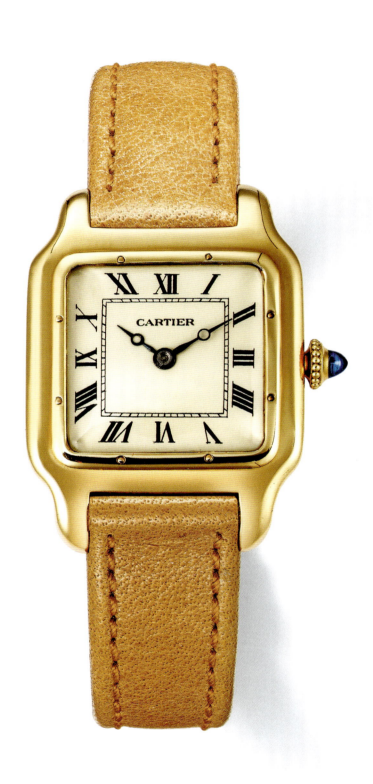

Santos
Cartier 1904

The introduction of the wristwatch cannot be traced back to a single name, but Cartier can boast of being the first brand to regularly market a wristwatch in 1911: the Santos, which, rather than one of the many variations on the pocket watch, or a specimen conceived for military purposes, was a true original, pioneering model. The first watch by Cartier, and one of the first wristwatches in history, is characterised by the essential lines and proportional rigour of its design. This watch abandons the curved line that was in vogue in the field of jewellery at the time. The need to find a convenient visual solution to the aesthetic problems raised by the wristwatch most likely led Cartier to accelerate the company's movement towards the Art Deco aesthetic. The case of the Santos, in fact, is essentially square, with rounded corners that extend to shape the lugs, while the dial follows the shape of the case, featuring the slender Roman numerals that would become one of the company's aesthetic hallmarks. The bezel is also square, adorned with eight small studs, a detail inspired by the rivets used on aircraft cockpits (over time, visible screws would appear on the bezel). Another characteristic detail is the cabochon sapphire set into the crown. The Santos has remained in the catalogue since the first decade of the twentieth century, becoming a Cartier icon, continually renewed over time.

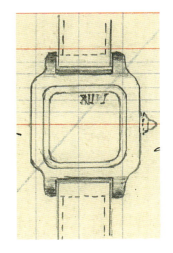

◀ **Wristwatch Santos-Dumont, Cartier Paris, 1912.** *Yellow gold, pink gold, one sapphire cabochon, leather strap.*
This particularly rare timepiece is one of the very first Santos wristwatches, a model produced by Cartier from 1911 onwards.
Round LeCoultre Calibre 126 movement, Côtes de Genève decoration, rhodium-plated, 8 adjustments, 18 jewels, Swiss lever escapement, bimetallic balance, Breguet balance spring. Cartier Collection.

▶ *Sketch for a Santos wristwatch, extract from a stock register.*
Cartier Paris, 1911. Cartier Paris Archives.

John Shaeffer
Audemars Piguet 1907

The wristwatch with a minute-repeater complication was designed by Audemars Piguet for the American industrialist John Shaeffer in 1907. The "minute repeater" complication was born toward the end of the seventeenth century. In this period, when illumination was provided by candlelight, watchmakers began to experiment towards creating (pocket) watches that could assist in telling the time when it was not always possible to consult the watch with one's eyes. A minute-repeater complication in mechanical watches, therefore, indicates the time acoustically. Watches of this type have an independent ring tone with two separate hammers, which can strike sounds in different tones, distinguishing between the hours, quarters of an hour, and minutes. Watchmakers usually use a low tone for the hours, a two-tone sequence for quarter hours, and a high-pitched sound for minutes.

Audemars Piguet was one of the first watchmakers to produce minute-repeater wristwatches, and Shaeffer, realising that his name consisted of twelve letters, asked the *maison* to personalise the watch design. The model had a cushion-shaped case, with the dial bearing the letters of the owner's full name in the place of numerals.

This historic model inspired the creation of the John Shaeffer line, which entered the Audemars Piguet catalogue in 1995, with various versions available for purchase.

Cushion-shaped case in platinum and yellow gold, measuring 31.3 x 31.3mm (1¼ x 1¼in), white dial with 12 letters applied in white gold to form the name "John Shaeffer" (the customer for whom it was made), white gold cathedral hands. In addition to displaying the hours and minutes, the watch also includes a minute-repeater complication.

THE EARLY 1900s —

1907

The 1910s

Approaching the Great War

The decade spanning 1910 to 1920 was one of the most shocking in history. Even prior to the world conflict that would engulf Europe and the rest of the world between 1914 and 1918, the period was animated by great social unrest. The political balance was growing ever more precarious due to nationalist tensions and extremist attitudes, while demonstrations by suffragettes, fighting for recognition of their voting rights and to achieve parity with men generally, intensified in both legal and economic realms.

At the same time, there was a great ferment in the world of art: the decade was especially intense, full of variety and dynamism, and characterised by a complex articulation of styles rather than uniformity. In this eclectic period, the sinuous, interweaving lines of Art Nouveau met with the rigorous, geometric lines of the art movements anticipating Art Deco. Prevailing among the wealthy classes in contrast to this aesthetic were historic *avant-garde* movements that had been developing since the early years of the twentieth century, which had a rousing, innovative power to them; these included Symbolism, Fauvism, Cubism, Futurism, Expressionism and Dadaism. In many cases, they were also fuelled by political ideologies, which would lead to a profound transformation of the artistic lexicon. These currents were also all conceptually intertwined with other cultural, scientific, technological and philosophical events that had a significant influence on society at the time and, indeed, would modify it profoundly. Sigmund Freud's *The Interpretation of Dreams* had been published in 1899, and the innovative readings of the psyche offered by Freudian studies influenced the work of the Symbolists, anticipating Surrealism. New concepts of reality, representation and memory

---

◀ *6 May 1910. The Duke of Roxburghe visits Buckingham Palace following the death of King Edward VII.*

emerged from the research of Henri Bergson, collected in the publications *Time and Free Will: An Essay on the Immediate Data of Consciousness* (1889) and *Matter and Memory* (1896), which also opened new paths in the perception of time. Albert Einstein's revolutionary theory of relativity, first published in 1905, suggested, to artists of the Cubist and Dadaist current, potential future perspectives on reality. Mechanical innovations in flight and automobiles fascinated the Futurists, whose aesthetic projected itself towards the new, just as it was intent on severing links with the past.

A geometric, antinaturalistic style was born of these trends, already orienting itself towards simplified shapes and broken lines. Elegant, accurate and precious in terms of material selection and other respects, this aesthetic influenced the production of home decor, artifacts, jewellery and, of course, watches. This last category in particular was freed from restrictive floral harmonies to embrace this new linearity.

A Fashion amid Elegance, Provocation and Precision

In wartime, the scarcity of available materials led fashion to bend towards a more austere style, embracing new demands for practicality and frugality and using a limited range of colours with a prevalence of dark shades for both men and women. When considering changes in fashion, not only in terms of its function but in its capacity for creative expression, Coco Chanel must be named as a protagonist. Chanel had opened a boutique in Deauville in 1913, followed in 1915 by another shop in Biarritz, where she dressed ladies who had fled Paris and found refuge in resorts. A great entrepreneur, she was able to offer clothing produced in one of the few fabrics available: jersey. Her garments were not "war clothes", however, but dresses, albeit rendered with a strong linearity. They were sought after for their workmanship and cut, with ladies of the aristocracy competing for them at very high prices.

Many men joined the army, and, from 1914 until nearly the end of the decade, they wore only military uniforms. Military apparel was not only accepted, but rather it was recognised as masculine and preferable to bourgeois refinements; the latter bordered in some cases on dandyism, an excessive attention to detail and care for one's appearance. For the futurist Filippo Tommaso Marinetti, the appearance of virility in a man enhanced his capacity for seduction, as the artist's writing attests: "There is no lover that a beautiful woman can have but a soldier, fully armed, returning from the front and soon again to depart. His boots, spurs, and bandolier are essentials for love. The jacket, the tailcoat, the tuxedo, and the frock coat are made for the seat, the armchair. They evoke the library, the slow defloration of untouched books, the green-shaded lamp, the fetid breath of moralists, professors, critics, philosophers, and pedants. These are, in fact, the husbands that I crown consistently thus: the enemies of divine speed, all."[1]

---

[1] F.T. Marinetti, *Come si seducono le donne e si tradiscono gli uomini*, in Pautasso, Guido Andrea (ed.), "Moda Futurista. Eleganza e seduzione", Abscondita, Milan, 2016.

THE 1910s

Immediately after the war, men's clothing would return to the three-piece suit. If at the beginning of the century the less-formal suit of a well-to-do man was worn only for lounging around the house, the three-piece suits in the early years of the second decade, dubbed "lounge" suits, were becoming more noticeable and more popular than the men's dress worn before 1910, establishing the frock coat. Especially after the war, a slow but persistent, more casual alternative to formal clothing began to appear. Trousers were tapered at the ankle and shorter, while collars were high on the neck and starched. The lounge suit was often worn with a bowler or wide-brimmed felt hat, though upper-class men continued to wear top hats. In the evening, dark tailcoats were paired with white waistcoats, and the tuxedo, though less formal, was considered an acceptable form of elegant attire. Born as a complement to military uniforms, the trench coat entered gentlemen's wardrobes after the war, and over time it would become one of the first unisex items of clothing.

One item would enter this revolution of taste and style to become the very symbol of progress and modernity: the wristwatch. While watches for men's waistcoat pockets and pendant watches for women were still the standard, the pre-war years were already witnessing a series

Tiffany & Co., Pendant Watch Necklace, c. 1910.
Women's pendant watch with circular steel dial, signed Tiffany & Co., with Arabic numerals and steel hands. Green guilloché enamel is applied to the bezel and blue guilloché enamel to the case, which features rose-cut diamonds in millegrain settings. Its chain is made of tapered links coated in blue and white enamel.

— THE 1910s

of newborn watches that distanced themselves from the usual rounded shape, as if to emphasise that the new timepieces were something beyond mere adaptations of the traditional. Thus began a new chapter in wristwatch-making. The market, however, was yet to be conquered. The greatest watchmakers of the time immediately took up the challenge: one needed to adapt watch movements by rethinking their dimensions, or their cases by making them more shock-resistant.

Aesthetics and Ergonomics

At the end of the nineteenth century and the beginning of the twentieth, wristwatch design was heavily influenced by that of the pocket watch: its shape was predominantly round, it had wire lugs where the band was inserted, and its case was fitted with a large crown placed at 12 or 3 o'clock. Several "hybrid" examples marked the transition from waistcoat pocket to wrist.

Master watchmakers gave their imaginations free rein in these years, creating small timepieces of various shapes for the wrist that gradually met the favour of the public – still a predominantly female one, at least in the first half of the decade. The world of the wristwatch at this time was full of various interesting objects due to the variety of processes, materials and shapes involved. This model of watch constituted both a technical and aesthetic revolution. The traditional round watch took on an absolute freedom of shape, becoming square, hexagonal, diamond or almond-shaped, always according to soft, graceful harmonies

Tortue wristwatch, Cartier Paris, 1919. *Platinum, gold; one sapphire cabochon; leather strap. Round LeCoultre Calibre 126 movement, fausses Côtes de Genève decoration, 8 adjustments, 18 jewels, Swiss lever escapement, bimetallic balance, Breguet balance spring. Cartier Collection.*

with a balance of line and volume. One area where watchmakers directed their work was ergonomics, since it was just as important for a wristwatch to be comfortable as it was for it to be aesthetically pleasing. In 1912, Movado introduced the Polyplan, a watch with an oblong case that was curved to accommodate the shape of the wrist. Its name was derived from the specific build of its movement, which was constructed on three distinct planes, the only way it was possible to obtain such a pronounced curvature. In the first decades of the twentieth century, watchmaking factories began to make ever smaller calibres (mechanisms), which were well suited to wristwatch cases' smaller diameter. Between 1914 and 1915, Vacheron Constantin created a small oblong movement dubbed *le tuyau* (the "pipe"), which was used to make a watch purchased by the Maharaja of Patiala. Watchmakers also paid special attention to the band – offered in black silk for ladies to bring out the precious stones set around a watch dial, and in leather for gentlemen – and it would become a central site of significant technical innovation. In 1910, Cartier and Jaeger created the *boucle déployante*, a folding clasp – also known as a "deployant" clasp or buckle – made of a set of plates and hinges that folded and locked together, ensuring a solid bond to the wrist. It was more convenient than the pin buckle (a buckle with a point, or pin, that closes like a belt), with the advantage of being securable with a single move of the hand, and it would become the most popular closure in watchmaking.

Even as European society was traversed by a series of anxieties that would be catalysed in global conflict, the wealthy classes still sought luxury items that made their lives pleasant and comfortable. The incident that would ignite the First World War came on 28 June 1914, when an attack in Sarajevo by Bosnian Serb student Gavrilo Princip took the lives of Archduke Franz Ferdinand, heir to the Habsburg throne, and his wife Sophie. The tragedy of the conflict, in which thirty-seven million people lost their lives, marked the end of the Belle Époque. It destroyed daily living in all nations involved in the terrible event, and, with that, suddenly and radically altered fashion and social custom.

Necessities of War

The war profoundly altered the activities of watchmaking companies, both in terms of productivity and what was available. Business generally came to a halt. Switzerland remained a neutral country, and this allowed factories to continue working, although in many cases

Girard-Perregaux, Watch for the Prussian Navy, 1889.
One of the first wristwatches made for war. A metal grille protects the dial, allowing for the time to be read. This was the base model for the development of military watches in the years, even decades, to follow.

— THE 1910s

Advertisement, 1918. *A wristwatch advertisement that appeared in* Signalling, *a pamphlet dedicated to British military officers published in London in 1918, edited by Captain E.J. Solano.*

they were emptied due to general mobilisation. Manufacturers were faced with a European market in crisis, not only because of the war, but also by the Russian Revolution of 1917, which wiped out an entire economy that had been important to brands of watches. Many of them began to produce watches for military use. Soldiers engaged in war operations simultaneously needed their hands free and to know the exact time: because one's watch needed to be consulted quickly, the wristwatch was adopted. During the First World War, planes were used for the first time for reconnaissance and internal communications, as well as for combat missions in the air: aviators, seated in the open cockpits of their planes, had neither the space nor the time to use pocket watches, and needed to monitor flight times, given their aircrafts' limited capabilities. Regiments on the ground, for their part, needed to co-ordinate their actions.

Military use of the watch therefore promoted the development of materials and technical solutions. One characteristic required of military watches was a robust case, which needed to withstand blows and be incorruptible. Manufacturers therefore used burnished iron as well as gold and silver. Protecting the dial was equally fundamental; many examples can be found featuring a grille with a hinge or snap closure to protect the glass on the dial, which was not yet being made from synthetic sapphire as watch crystals are today.[2]

Visibility was also a decisive factor. The Arabic numerals and hands of the dial, which was often dark, were therefore always clearly legible in terms of both graphics and size and, to make it easier to tell the time even in unfavourable light conditions, were made of luminescent material. Finally, the band had to be made from an inexpensive but tough, durable material such as leather or raw canvas. During the conflict, many heads of state decided to equip their armies, or at least their officers, with highly precise, reliable wristwatches that could provide an immediate reading of the time. Movado had already introduced a watch for military use with

---

[2] Sapphire crystal, or sapphire "glass", is a synthetic colourless corundum that is produced in a laboratory and is extremely hard and durable.

Longines, 1915. *Longines time-only demi-savonnette or "half-hunter" watch (with its dial protected by an outer case, with a porthole in the centre), dated to c. 1915. The enamel dial has fluorescent Arabic numerals. The numbers of the minute track are also shown around the porthole for immediate reading, without having to open the case.*

— THE 1910s

Trench Watch, 1916. *Watches made for the military had hinged lids on front and back to protect the dial, which was usually black, with white indices and hands for clearer reading.*

a protective grille in 1910, and, that same year, Longines began to supply Great Britain with a series of military pocket watches.

One of the first wristwatches intended specifically for men in uniform appeared around 1915. In 1917, the Royal Flying Corps, followed by the U.S. Army in 1918, selected Omega watches for its combat units. At the end of the war, these watches remained with the officers, facilitating their spread among civilians throughout Western culture.

Time and Movement

In the 1910s, watch manufacturers' workshops were renovated to produce precision watches with a chronograph function that allowed the wearer to keep track of situations involving time and space, such as the number of an engine's revolutions per minute, the speed at which a travelling person or object moved, and the distance covered in each given time interval.

Watch manufacturers took an interest in perfecting this mechanism, seeing the great potential it could have if installed in a wristwatch. The year 1913 marked a milestone in the history of Longines, and of watchmaking in general. That year, the company – having already introduced an early wrist chronograph in 1911 – introduced the first movement with a column wheel designed for a wristwatch: the hand-wound mechanical movement Calibre 13.33Z. This monopusher chronograph would be used until 1936, when it would be replaced by another movement by the company. This timepiece had a single button with which one could manage all three chronograph functions: start, stop and reset.

In 1925, Longines would continue the timekeeping experiment, introducing a dual-pusher wrist chronograph with flyback mechanism. The Swiss watchmaker launched a new flyback model in 1928, followed in 1929 by a watch with two independent push-pieces. All were made with Longines movements, which helped to define the chronograph's layout. Ulysse Nardin created a watch with a chronograph function in 1916: dubbed a "medical" chronograph, it had a graduated scale for thirty beats on its dial, allowing the wearer to detect a person's heartbeat. Breitling also developed chronometers with special dials specifically dedicated to measuring time intervals; in 1915, they introduced the independent chronograph button.

In 1919, Eberhard & Co. released one of the first chronographs to be worn on the wrist. It was a hand-wound mechanical model with a hinged bezel and caseback.

THE 1910s —

Eberhard & Co. pocket chronograph dating to the early twentieth century. *Burnished iron case, enamel dial with Arabic numerals and small seconds at 6 o'clock. Hand-wound mechanical movement.*

— THE 1910s

~1900

Hausmann & Co. – Baracca
Hausmann & Co. circa 1900

Sixty-three aerial fights, over the course of which he is said to have defeated thirty-four enemy aircraft: this was the record of Lieutenant Francesco Baracca, who fought his enemy in the air aboard his biplane, its left side adorned with the emblem of a horse rearing up on its hind legs. The pilot, together with a group of equally valiant companions, was part of Italy's *Squadriglia degli Aci* ("Squadron of Aces"). Towards evening on 19 June 1918, Baracca took off for yet another mission: a strafing on Montello, a hill in the Veneto region overlooking the Piave river between Nervesa and Montebelluna. He was not fated to return, however. His plane was hit by Austro-Hungarian  forces, and it was only after a week-long search that his companions found his remains. His watch, having marked the time of all thirty-four of his victories, stopped at the time of his death: 6.45 P.M. on 19 June 1918. It was a pocket timepiece produced by Hausmann, which Baracca had won a few years prior as a jockey in a horse race at Capannelle racecourse in Rome. He had had it attached to a wristband himself so he could see the time without removing his hands from the controls. It is now housed in the Francesco Baracca Museum in Lugo, Emilia-Romagna.

Memory of Baracca was not destined to fade, however. In 1923, the aviator's mother, Countess Paolina Biancoli, gave Enzo Ferrari permission to use her son's emblem. The prancing, rearing horse, its colour modified, has since then "flown" on Italy's most famous set of wheels.

◀ *Pocket watch, adapted to be worn on the wrist by aviator Francesco Baracca.*
▲ *The legendary Italian pilots, together called the* Squadriglia degli Aci *("Squadron of Aces"). From the left: Gastone Novelli, Ferruccio Ranza, Fulco Ruffo di Calabria, Bartolomeo Costantini and Francesco Baracca. The image shows Baracca's watch, worn on his wrist.*

Polyplan
Movado 1912

Movado, meaning "movement" in Esperanto, was the name the Ditesheim family selected for their company, founded in the early twentieth century.

The firm's strong, innovative spirit led to a series of technical advancements that left a lasting mark on the history of watchmaking.

One of the most significant of these concerned the development of a timepiece whose Swiss Patent, N°60 360, was filed in June 1912. This was the Polyplan watch. It is said that the model was born from a sudden insight on the part of one of the company's founders, Isidore Ditesheim, who wished to create a watch that was ergonomic, and therefore comfortable when kept on the wrist.

Its name is derived from the unique shape of its movement, which is built on three distinct planes to adapt to its case, curved to follow the contour of the wrist. This was the only method that could result in a curvature so highly pronounced, more so than any other curved watch on the market. Its case's characteristic curvature did allow for an optimal fit on one's wrist, and for an exquisite elegance.

It was a true revolution for its time, considering the distinctive facets and difficult work required in its design and production. This explains why, albeit with cases of differing shapes, this watch remained in production from the 1910s up until the mid-1930s.

Polyplan wristwatch in 14-carat yellow gold with silvered dial, Arabic numerals, a subsidiary seconds dial, and a winding crown positioned at 12 o'clock.

1912

— THE 1910s

1915

Breitling Chronograph
Breitling   1915

When Léon Breitling founded his atelier in the Swiss Jura in 1884, he also decided to devote himself to an exclusive and demanding specialisation: the manufacture of chronographs and meters. These are precision instruments intended for use in sports, science, and industry. Thanks to the quality of its products, and their continuous search for innovation, the brand not only accompanied an evolution in competitive sports and motor racing, but also the first feats of aviation pioneers. These aviators needed reliable, high-performance instruments and thus quickly adopted chronographs, first for one's pocket, then wrist models by Breitling.

In 1915, when it pioneered the wrist chronograph, the firm introduced the first independent chronograph button. In 1923, it perfected this system by separating the "start" and "stop" function from the "reset" function. The (patented) innovation made it possible to add various times in succession without having to reset the watch hands to zero, whether one was timing a sports competition or a flight. In 1934, Breitling would create the second independent push button to reset.

Watch with an independent chronograph button, introduced by Breitling in 1915.

Tank
Cartier   1917

In some cases, the war provided inspiration for objects' design, consciously or no, and the Tank wristwatch is one such example. Louis Cartier began to draft the first designs of this model at the end of 1916, the year that the British Army deployed the first tanks in combat.

When finished, the shape of this timepiece recalled certain parts of these "mechanical monsters" for combat. Its two vertical sidebars, called "brancards", were the result of formal research into the limits of stylisation, seeking to incorporate the hour circle into the lines of its bracelet. Cartier entrusted the practical side of realising the watch to Edmond Jaeger.

It is rumoured that, in a clever communications move, Louis Cartier decided to gift the first six examples, made in 1918, as a tribute to General John J. Pershing, commander of the American Expeditionary Forces in Europe, and to other officers. Pershing, nicknamed "Black Jack", had been one of the first generals to brilliantly co-ordinate ground troops using these very new twentieth-century war inventions, and he enjoyed a streak of victories. The watch model was put into production from 1919, and, even though only a few pieces were made in its early years, over time it became one of the company's most iconic pieces. The initial design was then joined by others: the Tank Cintreé with a curved, elongated case, which was made in 1921, complied fully with the dictates of Art Deco; the Tank Chinoise, inspired by Asian temple porticoes, was introduced in 1922; then, in 1928, came the Tank à Guichets, a "jumping hour" model, whose time was read through a window. There are countless other variations on this model, which has always been considered unisex.

Tank wristwatch, Cartier Paris, 1920. Platinum, gold, one sapphire cabochon, leather strap.
This especially rare timepiece is one of the very first Tank wristwatches, model produced by Cartier from 1919 onwards. Round LeCoultre Calibre 119 movement, Côtes de Genève decoration, rhodium-plated, 8 adjustments, 19 jewels, Swiss lever escapement, bimetallic balance, Breguet balance spring. Cartier Collection.

THE 1910s —

1917

The 1920s

The Roaring Twenties

In 1919, the Treaty of Versailles was signed, bringing an end to the First World War and restoring peace. The decade to follow, stretching to 1929 – the year of the stock market collapse and onset of the first great economic crisis – would be termed the *années folles*: the "crazy years". This period was characterised by a joyful, exuberant atmosphere.

A period of great prosperity began in Europe at the end of the armed conflict, supported in part by strong economic growth. After the war, the world seemed almost intoxicated by items of entertainment that technological development had made available: the radio, born during the Belle Époque, had been perfected, and the gramophone became more widespread, making it possible to listen and dance to jazz from overseas, while motion pictures with sound garnered worldwide fame for the wonders of Hollywood.

Paris became the undisputed European capital of entertainment, with cabaret and *café chantant*, where they danced the Charleston and one could attend the Revue Nègre. The latter's undisputed star was American-born dancer Joséphine Baker, who performed in revealing costumes that were scandalous for the era.

The period was marked aesthetically by Art Deco, an architectural and decorative style characterised by shapes and geometric elements, punctuated through use of colour. Deco would be an aesthetic typical of the applied arts until the end of the 1930s, albeit with the addition of various subtle differences to accommodate changing times.

Art Deco

The *Exposition Internationale des Arts Décoratifs et Industriels Modernes* (International Exhibition of Modern

---

◀ *Guests in elegant attire dancing at a formal party, late 1920s.*

— THE 1920s

Movado Ermeto watch.
The case is decorated with fine red and gold lacquer work depicting an Eastern landscape, embellished at its centre with a cabochon ruby. Its sliding panels open to reveal a square dial with Arabic numerals.

er to see the time while keeping the dial protected. Retractable models were made to be carried in the trouser pocket (no longer just that of a waistcoat) and in ladies' handbags, like Movado's Ermeto.

Introduced in 1926, the Ermeto was conceived as a travel watch. Its name, meaning "sealed" in Greek, derives from the fact that the movement and the dial are enclosed within an openable outer case, protecting them from dust and shock. In 1927, Movado made this model even more unique with an ingenious patent: a "rack-winding" system which wound the watch whenever the outer case was opened and closed. Alongside the traditional *pendentif*, a watch worn as a charm on a precious chain, and the widespread watch brooch, all the major fashion houses at the time were placing on the market women's wristwatches of all shapes (oval, rectangular, tonneau, hexagonal), embellished with gems, on pearl bracelets, or bands of velvet or moiré silk. New mechanisms allowed increasingly thinner cases to be made. In 1924, for example, Jaeger-LeCoultre created the Duoplan movement. Its parts were arranged on two planes, making it possible to design small-scale watches. In 1925, Longines introduced the first wristwatch that indicated a second time zone using a double hand.

Rectangular, *carré* (square) and *tonneau* (barrel) shapes were favourites in men's watchmaking, and many options were made available to gentlemen opting for the new instrument in this decade. Patek Philippe, for example, introduced the Gondolo in the early 1920s, which came with a rectangular, cushion, or round case, as well as the first split-seconds wrist chronograph in 1923. In 1925, the makers, ever dedicated to research, introduced the first wristwatch with a perpetual calendar and a wrist model with a minute repeater, a complica-

▶ *Purse watch, 1920s. Two-part slide-open silver case. Spring system for vertical placement. Hand-wound mechanical movement.*

— THE 1920s

tion that the *maison* had produced through its masterful skill in pocket watch manufacture.

Audemars Piguet also offered watches with a rectangular case, including one with a jumping hour, with the hour appearing in an aperture and minutes that could be read on the dial.

Production by Breguet between the two world wars also showed great variety. The maker introduced surprising creations as it participated in the development of wristwatches. These included watches with a square case and "cubist" numerals, sometimes set with precious stones, handless pocket and wristwatches with jumping hours and rotating dials, tonneau-shaped watches, and Art Deco watches, at times featuring geometric enamel patterns.[3]

"1929 is the year of overtaking: for the first time, wristwatch sales are exceeding pocket watch sales on world markets."[4]

Two inventions allowed the wristwatch to become the pre-eminent object for checking the time of day and timed activities; both would alter the concept of the watch forever, bringing it into the modern era. The first was from British watchmaker John Harwood, who patented a self-winding wristwatch in 1923, a technical revolution of enormous import. Beginning with Harwood's work in 1926, Blancpain created the first self-winding wristwatch. The movement of Blancpain's Harwood model had a power reserve of twelve hours, but its innovations did not end there: to seal the case perfectly, Blancpain

[3] BREGUET, EMMANUEL, *Breguet: Watchmakers Since 1775*, Alain De Gourcuff, Paris, 1997, p. 318.
[4] BARRACCA, JADER - NEGRETTI, GIANPIERO - NENCINI, FRANCO, *Le temps de Cartier*, Wrist International, Milan, 1989, p. 135.

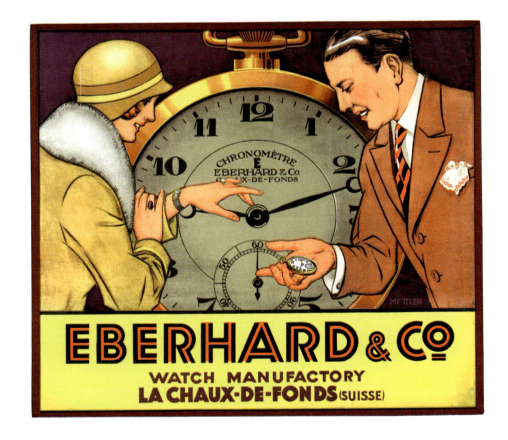

Eberhard advertisement.
An elegant advertisement by Eberhard with a graphic style typical of the 1920s. Wristwatches are marketed for ladies, pocket watches for gentlemen.

Rolex, Daily Mail, **1927.**
An advertisement that appeared in the Daily Mail *in 1927 to celebrate the crossing of the English Channel by swimmer Mercedes Gleitze, endorsing the Oyster waterproof watch.*

— THE 1920s

and Harwood eliminated the winding crown and introduced a system for setting the time by turning the bezel. The second extraordinary conception was equally innovative. Its patent, filed in 1926 by Rolex, concerned the first waterproof case, named the Oyster. Two fundamental innovations made the Oyster case watertight: an ingenious system of a screwed-down case back and bezel, and a newly patented winding crown. All that was needed to hermetically seal the case was to screw in its crown.

In 1931, the same Geneva-based company introduced the self-winding mechanism, with a rotor that pivoted three hundred and sixty degrees: the Perpetual. The combination of the automatic movement and the water-resistant case would serve as a model for all sports watches to come.

Aerial Explorers

Parallel to experimenting with form and elegance as well as underwater challenges in the field of watchmaking, work to achieve chronographic precision continued.

From 1919, Longines became the official timekeeper of the *Fédération aéronautique internationale* (World Air Sports Federation). The brand, whose emblem was a winged hourglass, from then on would join the world's most famous aviation pioneers in their great feats, earning the title of "The World's Most Honored Watch", a slogan quoted in its advertising campaigns at the time. Longines chronometers and chronographs were used in various raids and aerial crossings, including the flight by Richard Evelyn Byrd and Floyd Bennet to the North

Charles Lindbergh. *On 20 and 21 May 1927, Lindbergh made the first solo non-stop transatlantic flight, becoming one of the most acclaimed aviators in history.*
In 1933, he and his wife Anne carried out a 47,000-km (30,000-mile) aerial survey of four continents.

Pole, as well as Umberto Nobile, Roald Amundsen and Lincoln Ellsworth's aerial North Pole expedition in 1926. Two Longines chronometers were aboard the *Graf Zeppelin* airship that travelled around the world in thirty-five days in

This design, signed by the famous aviator, illustrates the information he provided to watchmakers in order to facilitate telling the time and other time-related measurements.

1929, and stopwatches and chronographs from the Saint-Imier firm were also used by American pilot Amelia Earhart, who in 1932 was the first woman to perform a solo transatlantic flight.

A significant event in Longines' history is their collaboration with the world's best-known aviator, Charles Lindbergh, who in 1927 made a memorable non-stop solo flight from New York to Paris aboard his plane, the *Spirit of St. Louis*. Following the historic feat – timed by Longines – which connected New York and Paris for the first time in 33 hours and 30 minutes, Charles Lindbergh designed the Hour Angle watch, which was later produced by Longines. With this watch, a plane's geographical position (longitude) could be calculated using a sextant and the stars. In 1927, Longines created another watch specifically for aviators: the Second-Setting watch, designed by U.S. Navy officer P. V. H. Weems, which allowed the seconds to be perfectly synchronised using a radio time signal. Lindbergh collaborated with Longines to introduce improvements to this model for certain needs in flight navigation.

In 1933, Lindbergh decided to embark on a survey of potential airways along the "Great Circle", this time accompanied by his wife Anne Morrow Lindbergh. The young couple left New York for a 47,000-kilometre (30,000-mile) flight. The equipment the pilot brought along to complete his long expedition included a Longines wrist chronograph specially created by the watchmaker for the adventure.

— THE 1920s

Gondolo
Patek Philippe 1921

The Gondolo wristwatch by Patek Philippe dates back to the 1920s, taking its name from the prestigious Rio de Janeiro jewellery-and-watch retailer Gondolo & Labouriau.

The Brazilian boutique and the Geneva-based manufacturer had already begun to collaborate at the end of the nineteenth century, when the Swiss firm started making pocket chronometers for South American dealers, now known as Chronometro Gondolo watches. The collection at first consisted exclusively of pocket watches, then the first wristwatches were added in the 1920s. Carlos Gondolo and Paulo Labouriau were responsible for a highly inventive marketing project that contributed to the success of Patek Philippe watches, both in Brazil and globally. Taking advantage of their exclusivity, the two partners created a collectors' club connected to an innovative sales system, the *Plano do Club Patek Philippe*. The "plan" allowed interested customers to purchase a watch by paying for it in seventy-nine weekly installments. The number of weeks was not accidental; the price of a timepiece was 790 Swiss francs, so the buyer would pay in weekly installments of ten francs. In addition, once a week for seventy-nine weeks, the buyer could participate in a draw. The person whose name was drawn was made the rightful owner of the watch that had been ordered, at the price of the installments paid up to that date.

The club had quickly become very popular, so much so that it had almost two hundred locations throughout the country. During this period of collaboration between the boutique and the Geneva-based manufacturer, Brazilian sales accounted for about one third of the company's turnover. Today, the Patek Philippe Gondolo collection includes a series of wristwatches with cases inspired by Art Deco in round, square, rectangular, tonneau or cushion (also known as the *carré cambré*, or "curved square") shapes.

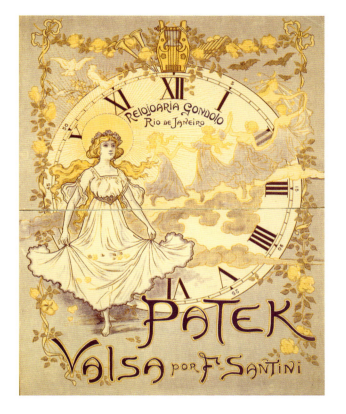

Chronometro Gondolo with tonneau-shaped gold case and silver-plated dial, with Arabic numerals and steel, pear-shaped hands.

Automatic Wristwatch
Harwood 1923

A mechanical watch is equipped with a movement consisting of various components. For the mechanism to work, it must be wound daily. Winding is done by means of the crown. The invention of the automatic watch is attributed to English watchmaker John Harwood, who obtained a patent in 1923 for a movement that did not require winding. A mechanical movement defined as "automatic" is equipped with a system that allows for continuous winding of the wristwatch via the movements of the person wearing it. An eccentric weight in the shape of a crescent, which always tends to rotate downwards by force of gravity at every slight swing of the watch, is connected to a series of gears that transmit their rotation to the mainspring, storing the energy needed for the watch to work. In theory, an automatic watch would not need to be wound if it was never taken off the wrist.

Automatic watch with a round 9-carat rose gold case and a rotating bezel to adjust the hands, a snap case back, silvered dial, Arabic numerals, and blued steel hands. Dial and movement signed Harwood.

THE 1920s —

1923

— THE 1920s

Oyster
Rolex 1926

The success of the Oyster, progenitor of one of the best-known lines in watchmaking, is due not only to the product's singular characteristic, which was destined to make a splash; it is also thanks to the communicative ability of Hans Wilsdorf, founder of Rolex. To demonstrate the quality of its new case to the world, he arranged for an event that would attract a large audience and spread word about its novelty. In keeping with the new image of the sporty, independent woman, whose body was no longer hidden beneath the overabundant clothes of previous decades, Wilsdorf chose a woman to be the face of his waterproof watch. This was Mercedes Gleitze, a young Englishwoman who worked as a secretary but was also a professional swimmer. She was asked to take up the challenge of swimming the English Channel; and on 21 October 1927, the 26-year-old swimmer accomplished the feat wearing an Oyster tied around her neck. It remained submerged in the icy sea waters stretching between France and Great Britain for the ten-plus hours it took the athlete to complete her crossing. Once ashore, the watch was checked and found to be in perfect working order. Of course, this all took place under the eyes of the press, which brought wide appeal to the swimmer's record and to the new watch model. To celebrate the historic event, Wilsdorf also placed an ad on the front page of London's *Daily Mail*, relating Gleitze's achievement and the success of the first waterproof wristwatch. The young woman effectively gave Rolex its first celebrity endorsement.

In 1926, Rolex invented the waterproof wristwatch, billed as the "miracle watch". In jewellers' cases, the Oyster was displayed while immersed in a fish tank, to demonstrate its water resistance, impressing passers-by.

1926

— THE 1920S

Lindbergh Hour Angle
Longines   1931

In 1927, commander P.V.H. Weems designed an hour angle watch with a rotating dial calibrated to the second, which he patented in 1929. Charles Lindbergh added modifications to this fundamental design concerning the dial and bezel, which were covered by a patent. This is how the Hour Angle watch was born, produced by Longines from 1931. It was a simple but decisive invention, which allowed the clock to be synchronised to the second with a radio time signal via the outer bezel of the central dial. In the first decades of the twentieth century, these dimensions made it easier to read and use the watch in dim light, resisting the intense vibrations of the aeroplane. The large knurled crown also offered a secure grip for a pilot or co-pilot's gloved fingers.

The Longines Lindbergh was the first wristwatch in the world to feature a rotating bezel, an innovation that would later be integrated into many models, especially diving watches. The rotating bezel with 60 minutes or seconds first appeared on a Weems watch by Longines in 1934. Used in combination with a sextant and a nautical almanac, the Hour Angle watch made it possible to determine one's geographical position through a precise calculation of longitude.

Fitted with a large leather strap, Lindbergh wore the Hour Angle watch on his arm, or his knee, for greater freedom of movement. Longines produced a series of Lindbergh watches in the 1930s, then revived the model in the 1940s.

Hour Angle pilot's wristwatch. 47mm-diameter (1%₁₀in-diameter) steel case, silver-plated rotating bezel, calibrated for 15-degree graduations in blue enamel. Inner rotating disc calibrated for 60 seconds and 15 degrees. Longines hand-wound movement. The first watch with a rotating bezel.

1931

The 1930s

The Scrupulous and Surreal

The 1930s saw the emergence of an artistic movement that had arisen in 1920s France, and its guidelines were officially specified in writer André Breton's first Surrealist manifesto of 1924. Surrealist artists were interested in depicting the human subconscious – dreams, desires and hidden fears. René Magritte and Salvador Dalí were major exponents of this group. Both, albeit with their differing stylisations, dealt with the theme of time, something of which contemporary society was becoming ever more aware. Indeed, both artists would use watches as subjects and symbolic elements in their work. In 1931, Dalí painted *The Persistence of Memory*, his famous painting, populated with "flaccid" clocks. The melting clocks remind us that the passage of time is not an absolute for everything – humans, animals, inanimate objects, elements of nature; for each, it has differing significance and effects. The objectivity of time was being questioned, as living out the hours, minutes, and seconds is different from actually experiencing them, and the memory of a moment experienced is, therefore, equally variable. The clock depicted as being devoured by insects perhaps represents the restlessness that every person feels in the face of the inexorable passage of time. Magritte addressed the theme of time in his canvas *Time Transfixed* (*La Durée poignardée*) from 1938, in which a locomotive is suspended mid-air inside a fireplace, with a clock resting on the mantel. Magritte used tools that were modern for the time, like the locomotive and the clock, to emphasise the speed of life, travelling on a different plane than the speed of the mind.

These currents in figurative art seemed to cast an astonished gaze upon reality, virtually awaiting the global tragedy that would occur within a few years' time.

◀ *Rudolph Valentino sports a Cartier Tank in* The Son of the Sheik *(1926).*

By contrast, a less committed and more decorative art was also spreading through portraits, mythological scenes, and bucolic or floral subjects, intended for those preferring not to think about the crisis.

Functional Beauty

The current of Rationalism prevailed in the architecture of the 1930s. The origins of its aesthetics, seeking a solution to the matter of an individual's relationship with a modern society born of industrialisation, can be found in Germany, beginning in the 1920s. Between 1919 and 1933, the Bauhaus school, founded in Weimar by Walter Gropius, created a union of art and craftsmanship that expressed itself through a new language linked to industrial production, setting new aesthetic standards for architecture and modern design. The style of the Bauhaus movement was characterised by limited forms representing a well-considered functionality, its purpose to create beautiful and functional objects within everyone's reach.

The Bauhaus design eliminates the superfluous and returns to the essential, favouring clean lines, geometric patterns, and strict, minimalist shapes; these were mostly conveyed in simple colours, especially the primary colours (red, yellow and blue), or in the contrast between black and white. While many see the Bauhaus style as a continuation of Art Deco, with which it shares geometric and linear shapes, it was in fact radically opposed to the decorative excess that was in vogue in the 1920s.

These great designers created simple, functional objects that have become icons of design, testifying to the fact that aesthetics and functionality can co-exist. The birth of this school marked a historic turning point in the world of architecture and design.

The basic principle of the Bauhaus movement's design was that "form follows function". This assumption also influenced the design of watches, which were increasingly being called upon to respond to the practical demands of ordinary life.

The Hollywood Dream

Against the backdrop of economic disaster, the film industry emerged as a generator of dreams and a vehicle to escape life's difficulties for a few hours.

In the 1930s, fashion found a simple, direct, free and technically perfect communication tool in motion pictures.

One need only recall the fact that one film, Frank Capra's *It Happened One Night* (1934) caused a collapse in vest sales. In one scene from the film, the male lead, Oscar winner Clark Gable, takes off his shirt to reveal that he was wearing nothing underneath it: half of America's youth immediately followed his example.

Watches had become part of the world of cinema a few years earlier, when Rudolph Valentino, despite historical inconsistencies, insisted on wearing his Cartier Tank watch during his scenes in *The Son of the Sheik*, directed by George Fitzmaurice and released in theatres in 1926.

America had, in the years preceding, presented itself to the world via the entertainment industry as the new Promised Land, exporting its model of life through films, music and dance, promising freedom, wellbeing and emancipa-

An advertisement illustrating the Reverso by Jaeger-LeCoultre and how it functions.

tion. Most pieces from the formal men's fashion of the previous decade slowly disappeared. Suits were still worn for formal events and institutional work settings, and the tuxedo continued to be a top choice for the evening. Popular garments coming from sports activities included blazers and sport jackets, with flannel trousers and open-necked shirts. Casual clothing, consisting of sweaters and shirts with a soft collar, became increasingly popular and were to be worn during the day in one's study and sporting activities. Ties were no longer mandatory. As sports gained traction, they altered aesthetic conventions surrounding the body and fashion. A healthy tan from physical activity spent out in the sun was welcome. Tennis and golf, already popular in the 1920s, saw a surge in popularity in the 1930s, while polo was especially enjoyed among the upper classes. In the mid-thirties, the typical shirt worn by players, the "polo", was one of the most popular menswear pieces for leisure. In 1934, *Esquire* magazine reported that navy-blue polo shirts had reached "the status of a uniform" on golf courses.

In line with this sportswear, the fashion trend towards wristwatches continued to spread until it prevailed over the pocket watch.

A Variety of Shapes and Colours

As in the years of the First World War, the luxury market was less affected by the crisis, and the production of major jewellery and watchmaking firms continued to adorn the wrists of their wealthy customers. The complex economic situation, however, obliged the use of different materials for watch manufacture.

Already by the mid-thirties, and in the forties, very rare and extremely expensive platinum was replaced with gold, often used in combination with other metal alloys, obtaining innumerable shades. Depending on the metal that was used, one could have a pale gold ranging from white to grey, rose gold, or even a gold with blue or green tones. Two-tone dials were born, combining yellow gold and white, silver, rose or champagne-coloured gold, elegant in their essential, linear designs.

As in the previous decade, "shaped" watches (watches with a non-circular case) continued to be produced. Rectangular, square, tonneau, cushion or tortoiseshell models were still widespread. Circular watches did make a comeback, however, especially in chronograph designs.

This type of watch was specifically suited to measuring times in professional and amateur sports competitions, seeking records in the water, on land, and in the air. For these models, particular attention was dedicated to work on the dials' graphics, aiming for clearer and clearer reading.

"Swiss-Made" Success

The Wall Street Crash and the Great Depression engulfed the United States and much of the world. Together with the First World War, it was one of the first "global" events in history, and the watch industry was also affected. As in the difficult period during the First World War, watchmaking production was partially oriented toward a clientele focused on technology and engineering, such as railways, factories and military corps, as various nations were equipping their armed forces. Another aspect of production was geared towards offering items that were more affordable, most of them exported to the United States. Swiss manufacturers' operational structure and ability to respond to the needs of the market on the one hand, as well as their high degree of quality and ability to offer mechanical watches as luxury items on the other, allowed them to overcome years of crisis while also finding new market outlets.

One strength of Swiss watchmaking lay specifically in offering more wristwatches featuring chronographs, calendars and other such complications. In addition to conferring prestige on a model, these complications attracted new customers.

The Swiss industry was also structured with the formation of associations, such as the *Fédération suisse des associations de fabricants d'horlogerie*, founded in 1929 to defend the interests of watch manufacturers. The *Schweizer Uhrenmesse* (Swiss Watch show), first held in a dedicated hall in Basel in 1931, and the *Salon suisse de l'horlogerie*, its first edition opening in La Chaux-de-Fonds on 26 August 1933, were conceived as showcases for putting the most interesting creations on display. The first edition of the *Salon* attracted more than forty thousand visitors. Given its success, it would be held repeatedly in the years to follow.

Passion and Chronographs

Against the backdrop of a society in crisis, elites continued to follow their passions and dreams. In those years, there were automobile road and track races, motorboat races, and aerial feats, all sports practised by a small number of the lucky few. Amid many political and racial tensions, the Olympic Games were held in 1932 and 1936, occasions when the element of precise time measurement was fundamental. In 1932, sometime before the start of the Olympic Games, a watchmaker left Bienne carrying thirty high-precision split-seconds chronographs, all chronometers certified by the Neuchâtel Observatory, to take them to Los Angeles. His task upon arrival was to teach the judges how to use the devices. Up to that point, the timing of athletes had been fairly inaccurate and was not performed with uniform instruments.

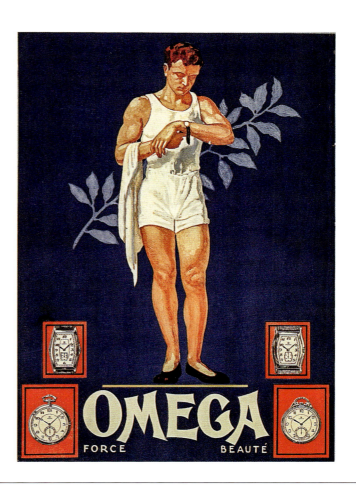

Advertising poster made by Omega for the 1932 Los Angeles Olympics.

— THE 1930s

Eberhard & Co., Split Seconds Steel Chronograph, 1939. *Enamel dial, push-button at 2 o'clock for chronograph functions, sliding button at 4 o'clock for reading intermediate times, and a push-button coaxial to the crown for split-seconds functions, with an external telemetric scale and spiral tachymeter scale.*

Timekeepers used their seconds counters to determine the final results, which were often the subject of disputes and negotiations. That year, however, Omega had been appointed the official timekeeper of the Olympic Games. At this point, the technical evolution of the chronograph had reached maturity, with a well-coded standard. This paved the way for unprecedented experimentation, giving birth to a great variety of models to meet the demand for capturing the seconds.

Breitling had already introduced the independent chronograph push-piece (button) in 1915 when pioneering the wrist chronograph, and in 1923 the company perfected this system by separating the start-stop function from the reset function. This patented innovation made it possible to add various successive times without having to reset the hands to zero, whether in reference to timing a sports competition or to measuring flight times. In 1934, the manufacturer patented a two-button chronograph with a second independent push-piece for resetting.

Longines had already produced its first flyback chronographs (with a modified Calibre 13.33Z) for pilots' wrists in 1925. In 1936, the company patented a calibre for the wristwatch chronograph, the 13ZN, in several variations, with a semi-instantaneous 30-minute counter or a 60-minute continuous counter.

The 1930s were very fertile for Eberhard & Co., which introduced a series of innovations. The year 1935 marked the introduction of an exclusive feature in the technology of its chronographs: the sliding button positioned at 4 o'clock for stopping and restarting the chronograph, without the need for resetting. The system allowed for an easy measurement of several intermediate times while simultaneously reading the overall time, which was ideal for all kinds of competitions. In 1938, a new model was added to the Eberhard & Co. line of wrist chronographs that included a seconds register on the dial. Until then, all similar watches had only featured a minutes register. In 1939, the rattrapante, or split-seconds chronograph, arrived, with two central seconds hands. At the Italian Naval Academy in Livorno, a steel Eberhard & Co. watch was the most coveted gift for graduating cadets. Within a few months, they would find themselves calculating routes and the war's ballistic data while at sea, often relying on the precision of Eberhard & Co.

Vacheron Constantin produced a series of chronographs, some with pulsometric and tachymetric scales.

Longines, Stainless Steel Flyback Chronograph Wristwatch with Registers, c. 1936. *13ZN hand-wound movement, silvered dial, Arabic numerals, two subsidiary dials for constant seconds and 30-minute register, polished and satin-finished case with unique, articulated lugs.*

The Man Who Loved Speed

The first Rolex chronographs, advertised since the 1930s, were designed exclusively as technical and functional instruments, and they were in fact chosen above all by engineers, chemists, architects, officials and sportsmen as a tool for work that could guarantee a high degree of precision and reliability. It is for this reason that they were produced in very limited quantities, which renders them all the more precious today.

Among the first Oyster Perpetuals made in the 1930s, one model that garnered success had a rotor attached to the movement, and its case back needed to be more rounded to accommodate it. This is why it was given the nickname of "Bubbleback", or the *ovetto* ("little egg"). In 1931, Rolex introduced and patented the world's first self-winding mechanism with a Perpetual rotor. This device is the progenitor of all modern automatic watches.

One Rolex Oyster was the watch of Sir Malcolm Campbell, who broke the world record for land speed nine times between 1924 and 1935, including five times at Daytona Beach, Florida, where the famous racetrack was later built. On 4 September 1935, at the wheel of the Blue Bird – and with a Rolex watch on his wrist – the speed king set a record of three hundred miles per hour at the Bonneville Salt Flats in Utah, becoming the first person to acheive that speed on land.

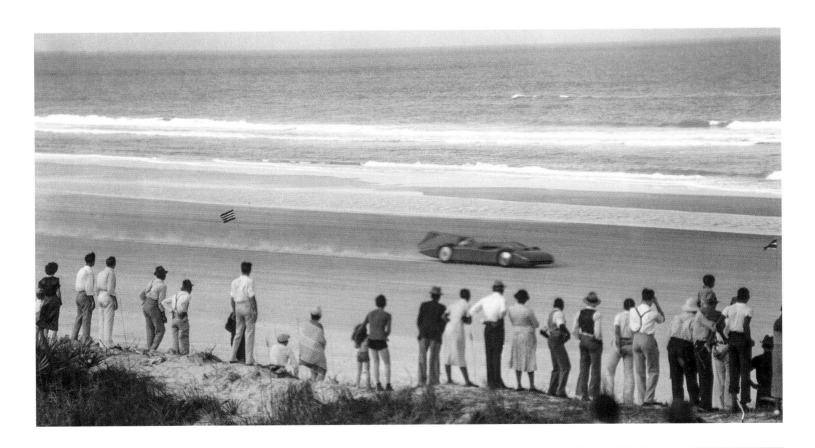

A crowd watches Sir Malcolm Campbell racing his car, named Blue Bird, at Daytona Beach, Florida in 1935. He wore a Rolex Oyster on his wrist.

THE 1930s

Sir Malcolm Campbell.

— THE 1930s

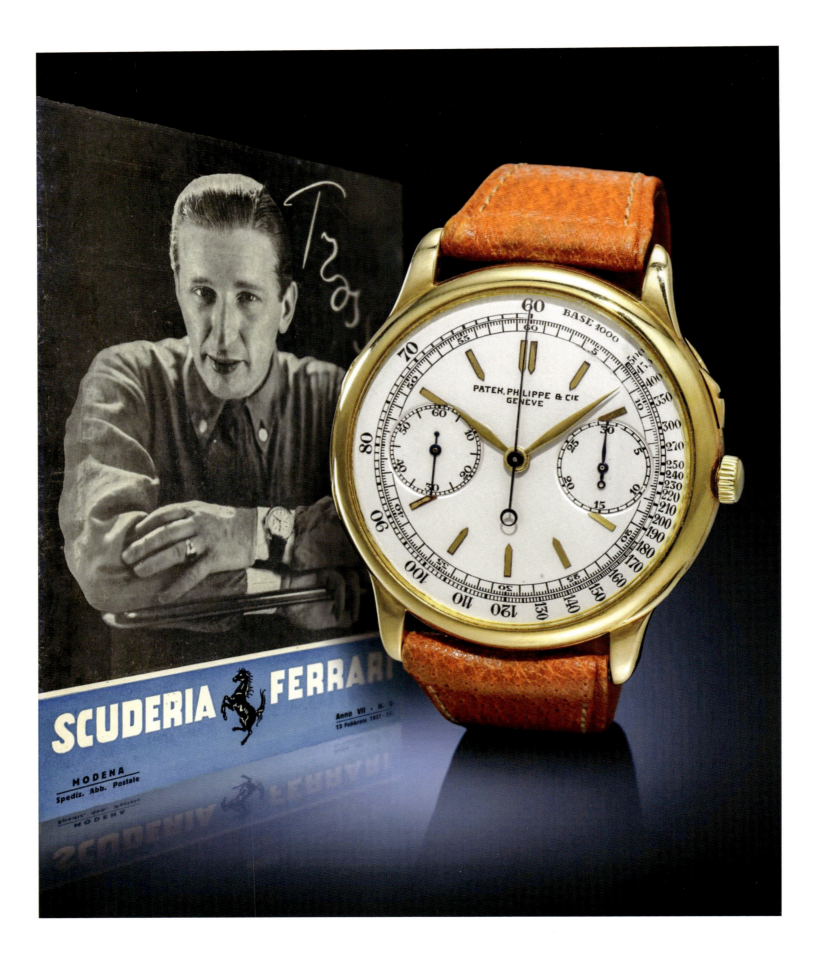

A Maestro with Style

As early as the second half of the nineteenth century, Patek Philippe was known for the excellence of its pocket chronographs. In 1922, the watchmaker had introduced a split-seconds wrist chronograph; and in the 1930s, he dedicated himself to the development of this type of watch, but always in limited quantities. These are unique pieces in some cases, limited editions in others. The reference 130 was produced from 1934 until about 1964: the model was enormously successful, made in yellow gold, rose gold, and steel.

Other successful chronographs included the reference 530 and the reference 553, both introduced in 1937, which were available in certain aesthetic variations and differing sizes.

Count Carlo Felice Trossi, a top-level driver at the Grand Prix and president of Scuderia Ferrari in 1932, chose a Patek Philippe, almost certainly a unique piece, to record times during the competitions where he loved to test himself. Research from Sotheby's describes the specimen accompanied by an extract from the archival material confirming its date of production in 1925 and its sale on 26 March 1932. According to the auction house, it is one of the Geneva-based watchmaker's first watches with horizontal registers; prior to this model, registers were usually positioned vertically on watch dials, echoing the more common style of pocket watches. A publication from Scuderia Ferrari shows Count Trossi wearing the watch in 1937: it is probably one of the first instances of a wristwatch being worn over a shirt cuff.

A Challenge at the Polo Club

History has it that the Swiss businessman and commercial agent for Jaeger-LeCoultre, César de Trey, was in India in 1930, then a British colony. The game of polo was widely practised in the clubs of His Majesty's officers; not even during the games, which were often intense to the point of physical altercation, did players go without their watches. Most of the time, these could not withstand the struggle between riders and ended up broken. Once back in Switzerland, the businessman informed Jacques-David LeCoultre of the need to create a durable timepiece. He commissioned the French designer René-Alfred Chauvot to develop a proposal for making the watch as resistant to breakage as possible. Thus was born a watch destined to become a classic: the Reverso. The aviator Amelia Earhart, who in 1935 made her famous non-stop solo flight from Mexico City to New York, had the map of her long itinerary engraved on the back of her Reverso in celebration of the feat. This is how the back of a watch case quickly became a privileged space on which to engrave messages, secret or not.

◀ *Despite the large 46mm (1¾in) case size, the Patek Philippe Trossi is perfectly proportioned. Its large dial houses a clearly visible tachymeter scale, which, of course, was very useful for calculating the speed of cars on a track. The chronograph's hands (i.e., the central chronograph seconds hand and the minute hand) are both moon-shaped and made of blued-steel, to clearly separate them from the gold hands and the straight blued steel constant seconds hand. The flat baton numerals applied are characteristic of the early 1930s.*

— THE 1930s

Prince
Rolex 1928

The Prince, introduced by Rolex in 1928, was well known among models with a pulsometric scale. It would almost immediately be known as the "Doctor's Watch". Of a rectangular shape, the watch had a larger dial at the top for the hours and minutes, and a small dial for the seconds below. This made it easier for a doctor to measure a patient's heart rate. The Prince was sold with two different cases, one that was more rectangular (Classic) and the other with more rounded edges (Brancard). Rolex produced the model in different materials: yellow gold, silver, platinum, or a two-tone combination of metals. To these models Rolex added the Railway Prince, its design inspired by the shape of a locomotive. The jump-hour model of the Prince showed only the minute hand in the upper dial, while the hour could be read as a numeral (1–12) through a window positioned at 12 o'clock on the lower dial. Years later, this invention would provide inspiration for the development of the Rolex Datejust. Watches of this type were so precious that in the 1930s, the price of a Rolex Prince was roughly equal to that of a car.

Railway Prince wristwatch with rectangular case (length 42mm/1⁷⁄₁₀in, width 22mm/⁵⁄₈in), case and dial in white and yellow gold

THE 1930s —

1928

— THE 1930s

1931

Reverso
Jaeger-LeCoultre   1931

Inspired by Art Deco designs, yet already oriented towards function, the Reverso perfectly embodied the spirit of its time: an exuberant modernity, introducing a radically new aesthetic language. In a world where silver dials prevailed, the original Reverso models featured a black dial with contrasting hour markers. The black dial was described as having excellent legibility and dubbed "the dial of the future". Almost immediately, variations in aesthetics began to appear with lacquer dials of various colours: bright red, brown, burgundy or blue, rendering the Reverso even more modern and distinctive. Its distinguishing characteristics come from the essential features of its design: horizontal decorative motifs emphasise the case's rectilinear arrangement, and its triangular lugs appear to be an extension of the case itself. It adapts so perfectly to its carrier as to, at first glance, conceal the fact that it can be turned over. The relationship between the length and width of the case is based on the golden ratio, a unique mathematical calculation defined by the ancient Greeks that is instinctively pleasing to the human eye when applied to proportions. From the beginning, cases made of various metals and models of smaller proportions were offered for women to wear on a cordonnet bracelet or as a pendant or handbag clip. In its more than ninety-year lifespan, this watch has housed more than fifty different calibres and had seven hundred dials, and its reverse side, born purely as a functional solution, has been transformed into a space to be decorated with enamel, engravings and precious stones, to the customer's taste.

The manufacturer faced a challenge when it came up with a watch whose case swivelled one hundred and eighty degrees into its carrier to protect the dial. The Reverso was created to meet polo players' need for a timepiece that could withstand repeated blows during play, but it was appreciated by all customers who loved clean, geometric lines. Its original design, distinguished by its rectangular case, gadroons, baton indices, and sword hands, has been revised over the years while never altering its essential design.

— THE 1930s

Calatrava
Patek Philippe 1932

The emblem that Patek Philippe selected was the Calatrava cross, a Greek cross with four fleurs-de-lis, arranged in the four cardinal directions. Calatrava was a monastic–military order founded in the middle of the twelfth century. Its emblem signified courage, chivalry and independence, the characteristics that Patek Philippe has always wanted to represent.

Jean Adrien Philippe opted for the Calatrava cross in 1887. He was drawn to its ornamentation and to the way it embodied Patek Philippe's values, including the long-term vision of its philosophy as a business.

The emblem's registration was renewed and extended on 25 January 1908, explicitly named the Calatrava Cross, serving as the distinctive symbol of Patek Philippe.

In 1932, the name of Calatrava would for the first time be associated with a Patek Philippe timepiece, inspired by the modernist aesthetic of the Bauhaus. The original model, whose technical name was the reference 96, sought to embody the very definition of a wristwatch: a perfectly circular watch, whose sole purpose was to tell the time. The white dial highlighted its elongated, triangular dauphine hands and bar indices, and the movement was manually wound. The first Calatrava watches had a diameter of just 30.5mm ($1^{13}/_{64}$in). It was very small compared to men's wristwatches of the time, but many generations of Calatrava designs have descended from the reference 96. The first variation on the 96 model was produced in 1934 and introduced a bezel with double Clous de Paris guilloché design, which would become a constant in subsequent productions. Historic milestones in the Calatrava's evolution include the introduction of the reference 3796 in 1982 (diameter 31mm/$1^{7}/_{32}$in), the reference 3919 (diameter 33.5mm/$1^{5}/_{16}$in) in 1985, and the reference 5107 (diameter 37mm/$1^{1}/_{2}$in) in 2000.

The first Calatrava was born in 1932. Known by the reference number 96, it is distinguished by a circular case 31mm ($1^{7}/_{32}$in) in diameter, with a flat profile and squared edges. Its design is one of great formal restraint.

THE 1930s —

1932

Marine
Omega 1932

While most diving watches originated in the 1950s, an interesting experiment was launched in the early 1930s. Omega first patented and introduced the Marine in 1932: it was the first watch specifically tested and approved for diving to significant depths. As a watch from the Art Deco period, it features a rectangular case. This unmistakable aesthetic feature, however, was joined by a series of revolutionary construction principles that guaranteed its water resistance: a double case made of Staybrite stainless steel or gold to protect its mechanism, a scratch-resistant sapphire crystal that allowed for good reading even while underwater, its seawater-resistant seal skin strap, the foldable buckle that allowed the band to be extended.

In 1936, the Marine was submerged in Lake Geneva to a depth of 73 metres (239 feet), and in 1937 it was officially certified by the Swiss Laboratory for Horology to withstand pressures of up to 135 metres (443 feet).

The Marine was appreciated by diving professionals and underwater explorers.

Omega's Marine was the first watch capable of being worn while scuba diving. Thanks to one case that fits inside another, it was able to withstand the pressure. The case design is inspired by Art Deco shapes.

— THE 1930s

1934

Perpetual Calendar and Moon Phases
Breguet 1934

This watch by Breguet, realised in 1929 and sold in 1934, is of historic significance, being the first Breguet wristwatch ever made with an instantaneous perpetual calendar. It is most probably also the first wristwatch to have a perpetual calendar without using a pocket-watch movement. The perpetual calendar is a highly complex mechanism made up of about one hundred components. It is rendered all the more complicated with the addition of the instantaneous "jump" system, which advances all the functions of the calendar at the same time, using a single lever. Manufacturing such a system for the considerably small movement of a wristwatch requires an extraordinarily high standard of workmanship.

The watch was sold to Monsieur Jean Dollfus on 28 February 1934, for the sum of 11,000 francs.

Jean Dollfus and his brother Louis were descendants of an important family of industrialists in the French textile industry. Both were passionate watch collectors and regular patrons of Breguet.

According to the inscription engraved on the back of this watch, the specimen was given to Louis by his brother Jean for having reached "five hundred hours of flight", a number beyond which a pilot is considered an "expert". Louis, an engineer and sportsman, was one of the first licensed aviators in France. He was also an avid sportscar driver and participated in the 24 Hours of Le Mans in 1926.

In 1997, Breguet patented a wristwatch movement with a straight-line perpetual calendar.

Wristwatch with instantaneous perpetual calendar and moon phases, tonneau-shaped case in white gold, 26 x 39mm (1 x 1½in), matt silvered dial, Breguet numerals, blued-steel Breguet hands, aperture for moon phases, three subsidiary dials for the day, month and date with constant seconds.

Portugieser
IWC Schaffhausen 1939

If the measurement of time is essential to those venturing among the clouds, it is equally important for those sailing the seas, as an aid to measuring longitude and latitude. As one of the great navigating cultures, the Portuguese certainly played a primary role in exploration between the Eastern and Western hemispheres. Perhaps it was in reference to their traditions and the needs of their sailors that, in 1939, two importers of Portuguese watches, Rodriguez and Teixeira, turned to an important Swiss manufacturer from Schaffhausen in search of the best technology. The two asked the firm, IWC, for steel-cased wristwatches that could work with an accuracy equal to that of a marine chronometer. At the time, this could only be done with a pocket-watch movement, so IWC placed the movement into a wristwatch case. This is how the first Portugieser ("Portuguese") was born. It had a very simple design, and its case, measuring 41.5mm (1⅔in) in diameter, was quite large for the time. As a solid and reliable timepiece, it quickly garnered considerable success. This first Portugieser became the progenitor of a family of IWC watches; for over seventy years, they have thrilled enthusiasts around the world with their precision, size and sophisticated mechanics.

IWC's Portugieser model was born in 1939, uniting the characteristics of a traditional nautical instrument with modern design and innovative mechanics.

THE 1930s —

1939

The 1940s

Art and Politics

By the 1940s, the Rationalist architecture that had arisen in prior decades contained multiple currents, ranging from Walter Gropius's Bauhaus to the vision of Le Corbusier, to the creative work of Frank Lloyd Wright, and it influenced object design. Made up of simple, essential lines, Rationalism's common feature was its reduction of form to a simplicity that corresponded with functionality.

Conversely, Nazi and Italian fascist totalitarian regimes promulgated a monumentalist style that drew on classicism, glorifying national history.

If a certain art had a so-called "social function" and was a spiritual "educator" of the populace, in some cases it served as a mirror, warning of barbarism: one example, notable above all others, was Pablo Picasso's *Guernica* (1937). The Spanish Civil War was the forerunner of the terrible global conflict to come; during the course of the conflict, in 1937, the town of Guernica was bombed and destroyed. Picasso's painting of the attack, which cost hundreds of civilians their lives, depicted it in tones of only black, white and grey. The composition, with its strong dramatic impact, is a condemnation of war and violence.

Rationing and Rebellions

Rigid guidelines were set with the general rationing of fabric and raw materials: single-breasted jackets were a "yes", double-breasted a "no"; lapels and the number of pockets were limited, and less material was used in pants, with no cuffs. Men relied on clothes they already owned or even on uniforms from the previous war, which, when reworked at home, created a similar style to that of service clothing. Amid this context of severity, a completely new style erupted in 1943. It had popular origins, having spread in the Harlem neigh-

◂ *Artie Shaw, American jazz clarinetist, in a picture taken during the 1940s.*

bourhood of New York. The zoot suit, consisting of an oversized jacket with a wide tie, and trousers with a very high waist, baggy at the top and tapered at the ankle: it was completely developed around the idea of the oversized as if to challenge rationing, displaying one's opulence. It was an early example of streetwear, created by young men who bought clothes of different sizes and remodelled them at tailors' shops in the ghetto. It became the favourite outfit of jazz musicians, then spread to gangsters as well. These elements of exaggerated style – broad shoulders, high waists, wide legs, and wide ties – would merge into the style of men's suits in the following decade. Generally, however, a more casual manner of dress would spread in the postwar period, both in the United States and in Europe.

Military Watches

The war drastically reduced private consumption, while also, on the other hand, opening new market niches. Established after the First World War as strategic and functional tools for war operations, the specialisation of military watches became more and more distinct between the 1930s and 1940s. Artillery units, for example, mainly used chronographs, which were able to mark time in intervals, memorise the division thereof, and measure distances using special telemetric or tachymeter scales. Meanwhile, special navy units – divers, raiders, frogmen – needed rigorously watertight specimens whose glow permitted their use underwater or during night raids. Aviators used large models with functions designed for use in flight. Beyond their individual intended uses, military watches shared a set of characteristics that included robustness, reliability and perfect dial legibility; the dial was usually dark, with clearly legible indices acheived through its graphic design, dimensions, and use of luminescent material. Military watches also had larger case sizes than those made for civilian use. In many instances, moreover, they were equipped with rather long leather straps, which allowed them to be worn over protective military suits or, in the case of aviators, to fasten them around the thigh so they could be consulted readily.

Many of these military chronographs had oversized crowns and buttons, so they could also be used while wearing gloves. At major watchmaking houses, many models were created for navies, air forces and armies. By the early 1930s, Breitling had already become the main supplier of the British Royal Air Force, for which it had made onboard chronographs for fighter-aircraft cockpits. The collaboration would continue and become increasingly intense over the course of the war. At the same time, chronographs designed for pilots' wrists were put on the market. A model introduced in 1936 had a black dial, luminescent numerals and hands, and a leather strap with very wide attachments. Around 1940, the watchmaker released new models, including versions with two pushbuttons, some with telemetry scales. Return chronographs were designed for bomber pilots, equipped with an operating system with forward and reverse functions, oversized controls, and a large, notched bezel, fitted with a strap that allowed the pilot to fasten it around the thigh. The methods used to deliver these watches were both ingenious and daring. In the first months of the war, when France was not yet fully occupied by German forces, Willy Breitling, determined not to interrupt supply of chronographs to the British, went with some friends to a pasture in the nearby Franches-Montagnes at night, taking several cars. At an

A German-made V-1 flying bomb on display on Antwerp's Groenplaats in 1945, perhaps following a parade in the aftermath of the victory.

agreed signal, the cars turned on their headlights. A plane appeared from the darkness, then landed,[1] loaded the goods, and immediately took off.

Among the numerous documented orders from Eberhard & Co., there were two of special importance: one from Rinaldo Piaggio Aeronautic and Mechanical Industries, and the other from the Regia Aeronautica (Italian Royal Air Force). Piaggio – which created some of the most innovative aircraft designs of the period between 1940 and 1945, including the only Italian long-range four-engine bomber – received precision chronometers and counters. The Regia Marina (Italian Royal Navy), via the Navy's General Staff and the Embassy in Bern, commissioned Eberhard & Co. to research and produce a new type of chronograph for astronomical navigation. The idea came from a brilliant officer, Publio Magini. Together with this instrument, which would also bear his signature, the courageous aviator's name would be celebrated for a secret flight from Rome to Tokyo in 1942, a successful undertaking that pushed the bounds of what could be accomplished in flight.

One of Eberhard's chronographs was donated by the citizens of Antwerp to the American general Clare Hibbs Armstrong, who had provided their city with protection. Between June 1944 and March 1945, over five thousand dangerous V-1 flying bombs dropped down on Antwerp. These bombs looked similar to a small plane, with straight wings and a reaction engine, flying at 600 kilometres (about 375 miles) per hour and could carry 900 kilograms (nearly 2,000 pounds) of explosives, with a range of about 200 kilometers (about 125 miles). Armstrong formed a special defence anti-aircraft force, which was able to protect not only the port but the entire town. For this, Armstrong received a chronograph in 1947 as a

---

[1] GENOUD, HERVÈ, Breitling: The Book, Breitling, La Chaux-de-Fonds, 2009, p. 92.

— THE 1940S

token of gratitude, an object that remained very important to him.

Longines had made some watches prior to the war specifically intended for aviators: the Weems Second Setting watch, designed by U.S. Navy officer P.V.H. Weems, which allowed the seconds hand to be perfectly synchronised according to a time signal received via radio, as well as the Hour Angle model for Charles Lindbergh, which made it possible to calculate the position of an aircraft in relation to Greenwich Sidereal Time or Mean (solar) Time. Thanks to their precision and dependability, many countries' armed forces chose to use Longines watches during the Second World War. These included the United States, Great Britain, Canada, Czechoslovakia, Serbia and others, such as Japan and Israel after the war for example. Longines played an important role in military watchmaking, producing Type A-7 watches intended for aviators. Chronographs from the A-7 series were monopusher watches whose dials were rotated forty-five degrees clockwise to facilitate reading. Used by American pilots, these had a large case and met the Armed Forces' criteria for reliability and robustness.

1942 saw the birth of a model destined to become an icon in the history of Longines. This

The 18-carat gold chronograph donated to General (at that time Colonel) Clare H. Armstrong.

chronograph (ref. 5699) had a red central hand to count the minutes and was dubbed the "Doppia Lancetta" (or "Double Hand") for its two central chronograph hands. The model displays an additional 12-hour counter at 3 o'clock (cal.13ZN 12).

Hans and Rudolf Homberger, heads of IWC (the International Watch Company), had a passion for flying and were both pilots. Perhaps it was due to their time spent in the skies and association with aviation that IWC launched the Special Watch for Pilots in 1936. Having gained a reputation as a manufacturer with excellent technical features, IWC would continue to receive orders for military watches, even after the war. In 1948, the company built the Mark 11 model for the British Royal Air Force, with a hand-wound Calibre 89 movement encased in a soft iron inner cage, which protected it from magnetic fields. It would continue in use by the Royal Air Force for over thirty years.

While Swiss manufacturers maintained a certain diplomatic balance by supplying customers from different countries, German companies, which had been active in the town of Glashütte since the mid-nineteenth century, found themselves working for the *Wehrmacht* (the armed forces of Germany).

Over the course of the Second World War, the watchmaker A. Lange & Söhne was chiefly dedicated to creating aviation and navigation watches, as well as so-called *Beobachtungsuhren* ("observation watches"). Like all German companies, it was forced to work for the *Wehrmacht*. Many pilot's watches for the *Luftwaffe* also began to be produced by Glashütte manufacturers. Due to their high accuracy and reliability, designs relating to their movements were classified as a "military secret". By 8 May 1945, the war was almost over, but a final series of bombings destroyed most of the buildings belonging to the Glashütte watchmaking industry. In the postwar period, the German industry was dismantled, and the Ore Mountains area, as a part of East Germany, came under Soviet influence.[2]

In the mid-1930s, the Italian Navy set up a secret programme of new submarine activities for its nascent diving branch, including the creation of a special department for assault operations, which needed special equipment. The company Panerai in Florence had experience in both watchmaking and in the process of making military instruments self-luminous (radium gun sights, for example), and it was involved in the development of some fundamental technical tools, including watches. To meet the parameters required by the Navy, Panerai created the reference 2533 diving watch, made on a base supplied by Rolex in Geneva and equipped with a special Radiomir-treated dial to meet the necessary parameters for legibility.

Panerai experimented with these watch specimens using various solutions for the dial, employing materials such as Plexiglas, brass and aluminium before arriving at a definitive solution. This involved a technique which laid two aluminium components on top of each other, each containing a self-luminescent material (Radiomir) based on

---

[2] In 1951, the socialist government authorities merged all of Glashütte's independent watch companies into a single "Volkseigener Betrieb" (VEB), or Publicly Owned Enterprise: VEB Glashütte Uhrenbetriebe. In the following decades, these horologists would become the main supplier of watches to states in the Eastern bloc. Production policy at this time led to the manufacture of watches that were quite affordable, though in large volumes, along the lines of the Russian output of the period. It was only after the fall of the Berlin Wall in the 1990s that makers began to work independently again, relaunching various brands.

— THE 1940s

A collection of historical Panerai watches.

radium. In 1940, the reference 2533 was changed, and the reference 3646 was born.

THE PRISONER'S WATCH

One particular watch model was also related to the war, though it was not a military watch. Many British officers wore Rolex watches, and these were confiscated when they were captured and sent to prisoner-of-war camps.

When owner of Rolex Hans Wilsdorf learned of this, he offered to replace all the watches that had been confiscated without asking for payment until the end of the war.

Officers needed only to write to Rolex explaining the circumstances of their loss and to specify where they were being held; the watches were usually delivered to POW camps via the Red Cross. The credit helped to raise morale among Allied prisoners of war, since the programme indicated that neither the manufacturer nor its owner believed the Nazis would win the war (otherwise, they would not be repaid).

Some British officers who ordered Rolex watches in this way later became famous for tak-

THE 1940s

Produced from 1939 to c. 1945, Ref. 3525 was the first Rolex chronograph to feature a waterproof Oyster case. The 3525 was the model that Hans Wilsdorf sent to British military prisoners detained in camps during the Second World War. It is also known as "the Prisoner of War Watch".

ing part in a mass escape from the German POW camp of Stalag Luft III in 1944 – an event that would inspire the film *The Great Escape* (1963), starring Steve McQueen.

CREATIVITY RESUMES

Once war commitments were fulfilled, the wristwatch enjoyed a very successful season between the second half of the 1940s and the early 1950s.

Leaving aside the uncertainties and fears related to war, one could witness an authentic triumph of creativity, while two major production lines were now clearly emerging: sports horology on the one hand, dedicated to increasingly sophisticated performance; and, on the other hand, highly elegant timepiece manufacture, definitively bestowing the connotations of a status symbol onto the watch.

The Breitling Chronomat is one model belonging to the first category. The Extra-fort model by Eberhard & Co. is among the most coveted. After the war, a new creative direction opened up for manufacturing, and at the end of the 1940s the watchmaker introduced a chronograph model onto the market featuring a slide button for measuring intermediate times. Today, it is still very much sought after by collectors around the world.

Rare Dato-Compax watches by Rolex also date back to this period. The *maison* traditionally did not produce watches with complications, but models born in 1947, with triple calendar (date, weekday and month) and chronograph functions, were an exception. The "Data" portion of its name refers to the complete date, as two apertures at twelve indeed display both the weekday and the month, while an arrow hand at the dial's centre points to the date. "Compax" indicates the chronograph "compasses" (registers) at 3 o'clock (minute scale) and 6 o'clock (hour scale). The register at 9 o'clock marks the clock's continuous seconds. These watches had a high price and were produced in limited numbers.

Rolex introduced another model in 1945, on the fortieth anniversary of the founding of Wilsdorf and Davis (the company that later became Rolex). Its innovative design would inaugurate a line that has lasted up to today: the Datejust. It is distinguished by its date display, visible

— THE 1940s

Advertising for the Extra-fort watch by Eberhard & Co. in the 1940s.

through a window on the dial at 3 o'clock.

As part of the postwar creative ferment, Audemars Piguet's master watchmakers created the thinnest wristwatch in the world, introduced in 1946: its movement was only 1.64 millimetres ($^1/_{16}$ inch) thick. The hand-wound calibre was enormously successful, as cases could be made without the size of the mechanism imposing any constraints.

Longines was also active, both technically and stylistically, introducing its first automatic movement, the Calibre 22A, in 1945. It was first used in men's watches; then it was also often used in women's watches. "Science and elegance" were key principles of the communication campaign launched by Longines in 1953, shared by the so-called "Longines circle": an elite with an enthusiasm for luxury, elegance and precision.

In the 1950s, the Saint-Imier brand launched three models that are still in use today: the Conquest (1954), the Flagship (1956), and the Super-Compressor diving watch (1959), now called the "Legend Diver".

After the war, the Jaeger-LeCoultre workshops resumed their work, and in 1946 the company presented its first automatic movement, the Calibre 476. From 1940 onwards, they were part of the house's catalogue of watches that had a complete calendar, with date, day, month and moon-phase functions, that would remain in production for many years.

Highly prized were the creations of Patek Philippe. The reference 1463, a chronograph introduced in 1940 that inaugurated a range of high-quality timepieces, is still sought after by today's collectors.

In 1941, a line of chronographs with a perpetual calendar was also launched at the Swiss

Reference 1463 was introduced by Patek Philippe in 1940 as the manufacturer's first water-resistant chronograph. It was available in three different series and up until 1969 was produced in yellow gold, pink gold, and steel.

Watch Fair in Basel with the reference 1518.

Equally important was the reference 1415, which had been introduced for the first time in 1939. This was a model with *heures universelles*, a world-time complication.

Though very few examples were made, it would be the progenitor of a long series of watches, inspiring many to follow. An advertisement of the period bore the slogan "For men with international interests, it is indispensable."

— THE 1940s

Special Pilot's Watch
IWC Schaffhausen 1936

In the early days of aviation, watches had to be protected against dust, extreme temperature changes, and the intense magnetic fields generated by the onboard instrumentation.

In 1936, IWC introduced a robust and reliable timepiece equipped with a triangle index to allow its user to set the take-off time, an antimagnetic escapement, and a rotating bezel. Additionally, its indices and hands, coated with luminescent radium, stood out on the black dial, making it easy to tell the time, even in the dark. In 1940, IWC produced what would be called the "Big Pilot's Watch" due to its extra-large dimensions: 55 millimetres (2¼ inches) in diameter and 17.5 millimetres (¾ inch) thick. In 1944, it would be the British Army that made a request for watches, ones that could be used by different units.

This is how the so-called "W. W. W." model (British Army code: "Watch. Wrist. Waterproof."), intended for military use, was born. These letters were engraved on its caseback, while the arrowhead symbol on the dial marked it as property of The Crown.

The most famous Pilot's Watch created in Schaffhausen was produced in 1948. At the request of the British Royal Air Force (RAF), IWC developed the Mark 11 Navigator's wristwatch, based on the Calibre 89. Its movement was placed within a soft iron cage which was able to protect it from magnetic fields. It would remain in use until 1981.

IWC launched its first Special Watch for Pilots in 1936: even then, it was equipped with a durable glass, a rotating bezel with an index for tracking short time intervals, and an antimagnetic movement. The design of the dial – clear, functional, essential – has all the characteristics of a classic Pilot's Watch: a black dial, triangular index, and luminescent hands and dial indices.

THE 1940s —

1936

1940

Panerai
Radiomir 1940

Panerai's Radiomir watch was developed in the mid-1930s with the reference 2533 and modified in 1940. Since then, reference 3646 Radiomir has retained the original, singular technical and aesthetic features that have been passed down to the present day: a large, unusual cushion-shaped steel case with a diameter of 47mm (1¾in), highly luminescent numerals and indices, and wire lugs bonded to the case. The high-quality manual mechanical movement used was primarily a Cortebert/Rolex Calibre 618, 16 ligne with 18,000 alternations per hour and a power reserve of 36 to 40 hours. The watch was also equipped with a leather strap sewn onto the lugs of the case, about 30mm (3¼in) wide, specially tanned to withstand diving in sea water. It was long enough to be worn over protective clothing and secured with a special metal pin buckle.

In this watch, the dial's overlapping disc (sandwich) structure was consolidated, with the indices and Arabic numerals perforated into the upper part, made of anodised aluminium; this was to make the radium-based self-luminescent paste placed between the discs brighter and more legible through the designated openings. To further improve its legibility, the most frequently used layout of the dial had four large Arabic numerals at 3, 6, 9 and 12 o'clock and eight bar markers corresponding to the other hours. This timepiece led Panerai to become a regular supplier of watches to the diving departments of the Italian Navy. The watches continued to be supplied, with subsequent technical developments – introducing lugs that were integrated with the case, for example – up until the 1960s. As one might expect, the Radiomir model was kept secret by the military, like all products manufactured exclusively for defence departments. Today the Radiomir is an essential model in Panerai's collection

---

Introduced in 1938, the Radiomir watch has a large cushion-shaped case (diameter: 47mm/1¾in). Its dial was black to heighten the visibility of its numerals and luminous hands.

Ref. 1518
Patek Philippe   1941

Since its origins, the watchmaker Patek Philippe has distinguished itself in fine horology for its scrupulous pursuit of perfection through technical and formal excellence. These characteristics constitute the Swiss company's best calling card, as the company was able to develop significant technological innovations while also making small structural improvements to its most acclaimed collections. Among its horological complications, the perpetual calendar certainly played a central role. The first wristwatch with a perpetual calendar, by Patek Philippe, dates to 1925, made with a women's pendant watch movement from 1898. It indicated the time of day, the moon phases, the date, the day of the week, and the month, and it was also equipped with a memory for the different lengths of the months, including the leap year. The perpetual-calendar mechanism employed a complicated instant "jump" system, which was refined in the later model (1936). Perpetual calendar movements are able to display the months with their various lengths (including February, whether twenty-eight or twenty-nine days long). To account for these instances, the technicians installed a year wheel, cams for the months, and a sophisticated system of levers that allowed the date wheel to slide by two or three positions at the end of each month with less than thirty-one days. It is for this reason that the perpetual calendar is considered, like the tourbillon and the minute repeater, to be one of the "grand complications" of fine watchmaking. A series began to be officially produced in 1941 with the introduction of the reference 1518; it marked the union of the perpetual calendar with the chronograph and was produced until 1954. Yellow gold was by far the most frequently used material, followed by rose gold and, finally, by steel, of which only four examples were made. In 1985, Patek Philippe introduced the reference 3940, with an ultra-thin perpetual calendar.

Watch with gold case 35mm (1⅜in) in diameter, very fine lugs, and a narrow bezel leaving space for the dial, with applied numerals and elegant feuille-shaped hands. Dates are given through two apertures at 12 o'clock indicating the month and day, while the moon phase is positioned at 6 o'clock.

THE 1940s —

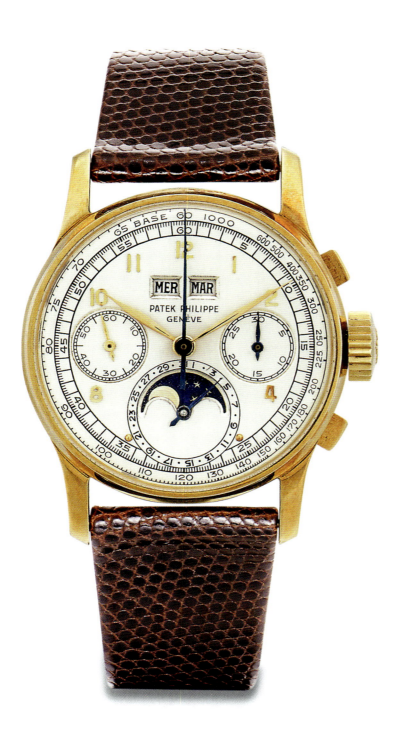

1941

— THE 1940s

1942

Chronomat
Breitling 1942

In the 1940s, the world of technology was dominated by an urgent imperative: that of measuring ever-shorter time intervals, as well as ever-smaller quantities and percentages. For those called upon to perform faster and faster calculations instantly, without the aid of special calculators, Breitling developed a chronograph that made it possible to also perform rather complex calculations. The watch was called the Chronomat. Its name meaning CHRONOgraph for MAThematicians, the watch actually had a circular slide-rule that made it possible to solve, thanks to its rotating bezel, a large number of mathematical calculations: multiplications, divisions and applications of the rule of three.

Hallmarks of this model include the case, with a curved profile, water resistance to a depth of five hundred metres, a screw-down crown with a push-piece, and the significant reinforcements protecting its controls.

It was introduced in 1942, and production continued in the years after. The Chronomat watch was conceived and then promoted as a model for scientists, engineers and mathematicians for recording times and making financial calculations. Many editions of the Chronomat continued to be produced in the 1960s and 1970s, only to be relaunched by the watchmaker in 1984 in a very different format: one similar to a pilot's watch, without the slide-rule. This new version was designed with the contribution of Italian military pilots.

Chronograph with slide-rule. A red circle with a 0–100 scale is at the centre of the dial, which can be used to read to one hundredth of a minute. The dial's Swiss cross and number 217012 refer to the Swiss government patent, granted in 1940.

Extra-fort
Eberhard & Co. 1942

Eberhard & Co. introduced the Extra-fort chronograph in 1942, and it would become the forebear of a line of chronographs with the perfect capacity to combine elegance and precision.

"Extra-fort" generally refers to the resistance and sturdiness of its cases, which were offered in steel, gold or gold-plated.

This was a manually wound mechanical Tri-Compax chronograph and an 18-carat gold case, which featured an Extra-fort edition of a 16-Ligne Eberhard movement, with a device for intermediate times: a push-piece at 2 o'clock with start-stop and reset chronograph functions, and a slide button at 4 o'clock, with a chronograph function that could stop and restart without resetting (an Eberhard & Co. patent). The dial was silvered, with embossed hour markers and a tachymeter that measured to one-fifth of a second. It was equipped with three registers. There is a 3 o'clock chronograph minute register; a six-hour chronograph register; continuous seconds at 9 o'clock; and a central seconds counter. The 40mm/1½in-diameter case made this watch a precursor of today's tastes.

In 1958, the watchmaker released the hand-wound split-second version of this model.

The Extra-fort was offered in various movement editions in the 1950s and 1960s. Today it is still highly coveted by collectors around the world. This is probably the watch with which the Eberhard & Co. brand is most identified internationally. A contemporary edition was launched in 1999, and it remains one of the manufacturer's iconic collections to this day.

Hand-wound mechanical chronograph with three subsidiary dials. 39.5mm (1½in) 18-carat gold case, silvered dial.

1942

— THE 1940s

1945

Datejust
Rolex   1945

The Datejust model appeared on the market in 1945 to celebrate the fortieth anniversary of the founding of Wilsdorf and Davis, the precursor of Rolex. It was the first chronometer model to display the date in a window at 3 o'clock on the dial.

The first model was made solely in yellow gold, except for a very limited number of rose-gold examples.

Three years following its launch, the Rolesor (steel and gold) edition was introduced, and, later, one only in steel. The name Datejust, however, only appeared on the dial from the early 1950s. In 1954, the company introduced the Cyclops lens in Basel; it was positioned over the date display, allowing the view of the date to be magnified. Since then, the lens has also been included on the Datejust. While the date window began to move a few hours before midnight in the first models, in 1955 a new mechanism clicked the date change instantly into place. The model had the shape of the Oyster case, a fluted bezel, and a five-row Jubilee bracelet designed specifically for Datejust watches. The Datejust is currently available in three sizes: 31, 36 and 41mm ($1^{1}/_{5}$, $1^{2}/_{5}$ and $1^{3}/_{5}$in). Each model offers a wide range of dials in different colours, finishes, and materials. Among the various options, dials are available with diamonds or in mother-of-pearl, with Jubilee, palm motif, or fluted decoration, a classic soleil finish, and laser-etched decorations.

Datejust 1945 chronometer watch with a gold case. Fluted bezel, white dial with gold indices, gold feuille-shaped hands, date display window at 3 o'clock, and a Jubilee bracelet specially designed for the model.

The 1950s

Return to Wellbeing

The decade of the 1950s opened onto a time of economic recovery. Paris was once again the capital of luxury; in 1950, festivities were held there for five days and five nights to celebrate the two-hundred-and-fiftieth anniversary of the Place Vendôme and to commemorate fifty years of the city's Métro, with magnificent light displays. Gala evenings were also returning to the palaces frequented by high society. In England in 1953, the coronation of Elizabeth II was an unprecedented media event, and thousands of people around the world could follow along, thanks to the growing accessibility of television sets. The love affairs of the international "jet set" were spotlit in the press, and women again looked to fashion. Pomp was once more on display via heiresses, Hollywood divas, and aristocratic women. One could enjoy such fatal encounters as that between Rita Hayworth and the Pakistani prince Aly Khan, son of Sultan Aga Khan, whom the actress married in 1949; or between Grace Kelly and Prince Rainier of Monaco, whose lavish nuptials took place in 1956. Elizabeth Taylor's turbulent relationships, first with Mike Todd and Eddie Fisher, then later with Richard Burton, were accompanied by the purchase of luxe accessories from the best jewellers.

Greater prosperity began to spread among all the social classes: the economic boom, along with significant engineering and industrial discoveries, profoundly changed everyday life. The invention and use of new materials like foam rubber, synthetic wicker, plastic and vinyl, with their unique forms of strength, lightness, solidity and flexibility, brought on the subversion of classic design paradigms. In product design, from car bodies to food packaging, from appliances to furniture, an aesthetic of curved and soft shapes was emerging, evoking comfort and

◂ *Icon of style and elegance, Hollywood actor Cary Grant in a photograph from the 1950s.*

— THE 1950s

"feel-good" sensations. At the start of the decade, natural colours prevailed: natural wood, white and beige with colourful insertions. The first daring combinations of optical and floral motifs would spread later on, still in pastel shades. Only at the end of the decade would an explosion of colour and liveliness, a prelude to the 1960s, begin to register.

At this time of renewal, newspapers communicated intensively with their readers, offering them information on how to dress, how to furnish their homes, where to go on vacation – how, in short, to create an individual lifestyle. Television began to embed itself in everyday life, to such a degree that it was able to exert its ever-growing influence on the public, giving rise to styles, trends, languages and obsessions. "Between the 1950s and 1960s, society therefore developed an economy based on personal consumption, with elements of personal and social distinction. New objects would then be purchased, which materialized different values and behaviors. The jewels, clothing, and cosmetics represented a more sensual female figure who valued herself, rather than invalidating herself for the sake of family. In contrast, the watch acquired a more marked sense of masculinity: it became an object associated with the work-

On the day of her coronation, held on 2 June 1953 in Westminster Abbey, the young queen wore a jewelled watch by Jaeger-LeCoultre. The watch was fitted with a Calibre 101, with a small rectangular case and a slim gold bracelet set with diamonds.

The mechanical Calibre 101 was introduced in 1929 to meet the aesthetic of women's watches. Shown here is a Jaeger-LeCoultre model with a Calibre 101 watch in white gold and diamonds.

ing hours, from both a practical and a symbolic standpoint."[1]

STYLE AND REBELLION

The postwar period brought a wave of optimism, happiness at new-found freedoms, and a desire to abandon the severe, dark years of world conflict – and this included one's clothing. Couturier Christian Dior swept away all the harshness of the war years in 1947, when he introduced the "new look" that would create a revolution in women's clothing. Italy began to carve out a dominant role in the world of fashion, thanks to the entrepreneur Giovanni Battista Giorgini, who organised the first Italian high fashion show in the Sala Bianca (or "white hall") of the Palazzo Pitti in 1951. His work provided impetus for what later became the "Made in Italy" mark.

While a true style revolution was occurring in women's fashion, men's clothing was less prone to experimentation. However, market development did see some innovation. Alongside traditional English tailoring, still highly respected for its accurate cuts and quality fabrics, there was an emergence of Italian menswear through figures like Brioni, Caraceni, Litrico and Piattelli, who helped to define an internationally coveted "Italian style". Film productions by Cinecittà, including *Roman Holiday* (1953), helped to portray Italy as a country of escape and good living.

In menswear, the suit remained an essential garment. Single- or double-breasted jackets with wide lapels were worn with trousers that tended to be tighter than in the previous decade, with no turn-ups, accompanied by slim ties. A less formal style was also spreading, however, which included separates with jackets that were more relaxed. Shades of brown and beige were the popular colours. On formal occasions, men continued to wear the shawl-lapel tuxedo, which was worn with a bow tie. The most significant change, however, was the growing presence of colour in details and accessories made for the tuxedo – ties and cummerbunds, for instance. Sweaters and shirts for daytime were also colourful. Men's fashion began to evolve towards more casual options to wear at weekends and on holidays: a cardigan, worn over a shirt, became a popular piece of clothing for men in the 1950s.

For those remaining faithful to the jacket, however, the blazer was introduced towards the end of the 1950s; it had short, wide lapels, and was combined with white trousers, light-coloured shirts, and a scarf. Young men's wardrobes were enhanced with pieces such as the wool turtleneck, to replace a shirt and tie, and the bomber jacket, a military-inspired jacket made of leather or fabric, with a loose cut and a zip fastening. The earliest "countercultures" also emerged during this time and began to influence men's fashion. Stars like Marlon Brando and James Dean in the films *The Wild One* (1953) and *Rebel Without a Cause* (1955) introduced a style of white T-shirts and blue jeans worn with a leather jacket, garments rendered iconic for millions of young people.

---

[1] SCARPELLINI, EMANUELA, *Material Nation: A Consumer's History of Modern Italy,* Oxford University Press, New York, 2011, pp. 153–154.

— THE 1950s

FORMAL EXPLORATIONS

The field of horology continued to create exclusive, limited-edition and custom watches, though many fashion houses would begin to produce lines intended for a wider audience. In these years, the watch achieved even greater technical precision. There were improvements in cases' water resistance, and, in tandem with a refined concept of function, modern design came to the forefront. A great deal of experimentation was dedicated to watch cases, exploring unusual stylistic canons in line with the aesthetics of the period. Makers played with curves with rounded, glossy surfaces, far from the rigid shapes of previous years. Moreover, though formal watches had previously needed to be of limited, understated proportions, in this decade their dimensions grew. An especially interesting example of this was a model introduced by Vacheron Constantin around 1950 with a *carré galbé* case (a square shape with curved sides); Italian collectors nicknamed it the "*Cioccolatone*" because it looked like a square of chocolate. Its rounded shape and generous size echoed the era's style, being in perfect harmony with the "zeitgeist".

Patek Philippe was also active in the realm of shaped watches, having made the reference 1593 in 1944; the company continued to produce it in the decade that followed. Easily recognisable by its flared outline, this model was dubbed the Hour Glass: its lugs, formed as part of the case, curve and broaden from the centre towards its outer edges, lending the watch its architectonic charm. Between 1948 and the mid-1950s, the *maison* produced the reference 2441: this model was called the Pagoda and nicknamed the "Eiffel Tower" by collectors for its resem-

Introduced c. 1950, this model by Vacheron Constantin was nicknamed the "Cioccolatone" by Italian collectors, for its resemblance to a square of chocolate. There are several variations of this design, including pieces with calendar and moon-phase complications. This example is equipped with an automatic movement and central seconds.
Pink gold case (35 x 43mm/1⅜ x 1¾in) with a silvered dial, applied square and triangular indices, baton hands.

blance to the base of the Parisian monument. Patek Philippe's reference 2442, produced from about 1949 to 1960, also reflected the evolution of taste towards a less rectilinear aesthetic, its unmistakable curves earning the watch the playful nicknames of "Banana" and "Marilyn Monroe". Its case dimensions (43 x 27mm/1¾ x 1in) were illustrative of the trend towards producing larger models. Working on its decorative schemes, the company also created a series of watches in 1951 featuring dials that had been decorated with subtly toned floral motifs in cloisonné enamel.

Of equal interest was Audemars Piguet's design for an asymmetrical rectangular watch. In 1953, the watchmaker introduced a model with a dial with set diamonds for indices. In the 1950s, Audemars Piguet also introduced a rectangular skeleton model (with its mechanism visible through the transparent dial). By 1934, the *maison* had already created a watch of this type destined to become part of the watchmaking tradition; and as the years went by at Le Brassus, several pocket and skeleton wristwatches emerged, sometimes as a jewelled version equipped with complications, even grand complications.

Patek Philippe's reference 2442 was playfully nicknamed "Banana" and "Marilyn Monroe".

Chic and Sporty

The Rolex Day-Date, launched at the Swiss Industries Fair in Basel in 1956, was an important innovation. It was the first watch to display the date with the full name of the weekday, using two apertures, at 3 and 12 o'clock, and the first from Rolex to boast a highly prestigious mark of distinction, the official "Superlative Chronometer" certificate of precision. A special band with an invisible clasp was created for this model, which was called the "President" bracelet, after President of the United States Dwight D. Eisenhower (in office from 1953 to 1961), who was given one of the first Day-Date watches as a gift. Sapphire crystal would be introduced in 1977, replacing crystals made of plastic and bringing water resistance to 100 metres (328 feet). Another important change occurred in 1988 when independent date and day setting was introduced. Modern models are available with weekdays in every language, and nearly all of them have a President bracelet.

During the Second World War, Rolex had produced a series of Oyster watches to meet the needs of the military and aviators. These had a diameter of 34 millimetres (1⅓ inches), making them slightly wider than the standard by 1 or 2 millimetres (⅛ or ¼ inch). These watches were especially robust, equipped with luminescent indices and hands, with good dial legibility.

These watches, worn above all by pilots in the British Royal Air Force, garnered a certain public success, and the Air King model remained on the market after the war ended, never leaving production.

— THE 1950s

Unlike the Datejust, which had been introduced a few years earlier and was produced mostly in steel, intended for a wide audience, the Day-Date was a luxury watch intended for elites.

From Professional Tool to Everyday Product

Driven by confidence in an expanding industry that was capably providing technical solutions in many sectors, the 1950s witnessed a series of explorations of the Earth, sky and sea, as well as space. Horologists raised their levels of technical achievement and were able to develop special watches tailored to the needs of specific professional groups. In a society where wellbeing and enthusiasm had grown following years of war-induced hardship, people began to embrace a sense of aspiration. Astronauts, scientists, pilots and athletes would provide original models for younger generations of the time, and they were destined to enjoy reliable, high-performance watches. Many of these models, created to meet specific needs, became icons of watchmaking and are still in production, even if modified over time with new technical and stylistic features. These include the 1952 Breitling Navitimer, intended for pilots; the 1953 Rolex Explorer, inspired by Edmund Hillary and Tenzing Norgay's historic ascent of Mt Everest; the IWC Ingenieur from 1955, designed specifically for engineers; the Type XX by Breguet, designed around 1950 for air and naval forces; and the Speedmaster by Omega, produced in 1957 and designed for professional pilots.

Underwater Explorations

It was in this decade that technical progress, the opportunity to travel, and a passion for exploration especially contributed to the success of sports and diving watch models.

A broader demand for practicality came with more widespread time for leisure and sports practice, and this gave rise to a series of diving watches. In 1948, Omega launched the Seamaster, which enjoyed great commercial success. In the development of this collection, the maker utilised technical solutions it had tested in the production of military watches, like the screw-in caseback. In 1957, Omega introduced the Automatic Seamaster model, which, according to a contemporary advertisement, was "specially designed for professional and amateur divers." Water resistance was guaranteed to a depth of up to 200 metres (656 feet).

Rolex advertisement celebrating Edmund Hillary and Tenzing Norgay's ascent of Mt Everest.

— THE 1950S

Advertisement for the automatic version of the Memovox, introduced in 1956.

In addition, its rotating bezel and luminescent indices made it possible to easily read immersion times.

In 1953, Blancpain introduced its Fifty Fathoms model, suited to the demands of sportsmen and military divers. In 1958, Breitling introduced its Superocean to the market with a one-piece case, intended for diving to great depths. The year 1959 was the beginning of Eberhard & Co.'s venture into diving watches, presenting two automatic models that were water-resistant at 100 and 200 metres (328 and 656 feet), dubbed the Scafograf.

In celebration of international scientific collaboration, 1958 was named the International Geophysical Year (IGY). Jaeger-LeCoultre honoured the event by creating the Geophysic Chronometer with an antimagnetic double case, which was also resistant to shocks and water.

In 1958, Longines presented its first true diving watch for civilian use, the Nautilus Skin Diver, ref. 6921. The steel case – 13.4mm (½in) thick with a diameter of 40mm (1½in) – was made by E. Piquerez SA and developed for a guaranteed water resistance up to 12 ATM. The model was equipped with a screw-down case back with a raised underwater motif and a black bi-directional rotating bezel graduated with a sexagesimal scale. It had radium-filled luminescent dots, indices, and hands and was powered by an automatic mechanical movement, the calibre 19AS.

ANTIMAGNETIC WATCHES

Watches used in industrial and scientific contexts, however, risked being subjected to electromagnetic radiation, which would negatively impact the precision and performance of the movement in a mechanical timepiece. For this reason, several watches were produced at this time with perfected antimagnetic systems for protection, among them the Ingenieur by IWC, dedicated to engineers as the category of professionals considered most likely to be exposed to magnetic fields; the Rolex Milgauss, made in 1956 to withstand magnetic fields of up to 1,000 gauss; Omega's Railmaster, introduced in 1957; and finally Eberhard & Co.'s Scientigraf, introduced in 1961.

THE 1950s —

The name of the Scafograf was registered in 1958, and the following year Eberhard's foray into diving watches began with two automatic waterproof models (waterproof at 100m and 200m/328ft and 656ft). They were the first of a generation and would become a benchmark for the brand.

◀ *A Blancpain Fifty Fathoms Milspec 1 from 1957 that was used in Operation Hardtack I, a series of submarine nuclear tests conducted in the Marshall Islands in 1958. In the US Navy's final test report, E.H. Lanphier wrote: "In summary, the experience with Blancpain's twelve diving watches during Operation HARDTACK has resulted in almost complete satisfaction."*

MODERN SPEED

In the 1950s, thanks to travel developments, the opening of transatlantic routes, the expansion of international trade agreements, and an increasing number of people – especially businessmen – operating globally, it became useful to have the continuously updated time in major cities "at one's wrist".[2] It was so useful, in fact, that the watch industry sought to develop mechanical solutions that could show the time in the twenty-four time zones simultaneously.

Patek Philippe had already created a series of watches with a world-time complication in the 1930s, in collaboration with the watchmaker Louis Cottier. It was in 1959, however, that the *maison* patented the complication, creating a watch that was much appreciated by the era's great travellers.

The Memovox was created at the Jaeger-LeCoultre workshops in 1950. Its chime could be used not only as a morning alarm, but also to remind the wearer of the appointments, schedules and deadlines of modern living.

In 1951, the company introduced another of its iconic watches: the Futurematic, the first automatic watch that had no winding crown. The inertia captured by its hammer rotor ensured that the watch always ran perfectly.

SLIM ON THE WRIST

Another trend that emerged in the 1950s was the creation of extra-flat movements, especially in the category of elegant watches commonly referred to as "dress watches". These were available with round cases of limited diameters, slim bezels, and leather straps, and were the preference of "gentlemen". In 1955, coinciding with the maker's two-hundredth-year anniversary, Vacheron Constantin brought one of the thinnest watches ever produced onto the market, with a manual calibre just 1.64 millimetres ($^1/_{16}$ inch) thick. An automatic movement that was 2.45 millimetres ($^1/_{10}$ inch) thick would be available from Audemars Piguet at the end of the 1950s.

During this decade, Girard-Perregaux contributed significantly to the development of precision movements. The company's introduction of the Gyromatic self-winding system in 1957 would help further the improvement of rotor-winding mechanisms.

---

[2] The first time zones on the continent of North America were established on 18 November 1883; and, following the International Meridian Conference held in Washington, DC in October 1884, the time zones were adopted as the international standard.

— THE 1950s

1950

Memovox
Jaeger-LeCoultre   1950

"The Memovox reminds, notifies, and wakes up." This is how a 1950s advertisement highlighted the merits of the watch that Jaeger-LeCoultre had just introduced to the market. In the years of economic recovery following the Second World War, the Memovox ("the voice of memory") was designed to remind businessmen of meetings and appointments by means of its chiming function. Characterised by simple, classic lines, this manually wound mechanical watch was distinguished by an additional crown, which controlled the alarm function. In 1956, Jaeger-LeCoultre enhanced the Memovox line by developing the collection's first automatic watch.

Three years after it was created, Jaeger-LeCoultre decided to garner a wider audience for its alarm clock, which had previously been limited to businessmen. The company sensed that the automatic watch was also ideal for explorers and other sportsmen. Later, it would turn to messaging that touted the "Memovox, for the man of action", to quote an advertisement from the 1970s, placing the watch alongside the Concorde, emblem of high-speed travel.

In 1958, to celebrate its 125th anniversary, the *maison* created two new models: the Memovox Worldtime, which indicated times around the world, and the Memovox Parking, which could be set like a parking meter to inform the wearer when their parking permission was expiring. In 1959 came the Memovox Deep Sea: it was the first diving watch with an alarm that could help divers check immersion times using an acoustic signal; then the Memovox Polaris, another diving watch with an alarm, was launched in 1968.

Watch with 35mm (1⅜in) gold case, gold double crown, white dial, gold hands and applied trapezoidal indices, and a leather strap.

Navitimer
Breitling 1952

In 1952, Willy Breitling developed a wrist chronograph equipped with a circular slide-rule that would allow pilots to perform all necessary flight calculations.

Two years later, the Aircraft Owners and Pilots Association (AOPA), the largest aviators' club in the world, introduced the design for this model as its official timepiece. The association's winged logo was engraved at 12 o'clock. This was the birth of the "navigation timer", or Navitimer. Allowing for all calculations necessary for rally flying or flying across long distances, the Navitimer was more than just a chronograph; it was a complete navigation instrument to be worn on the wrist.

Ten years later, in 1962, Breitling launched a Navitimer with a 24-hour dial. That same year, a Navitimer accompanied American astronaut Scott Carpenter on his orbital spaceflight aboard the Mercury-Aurora 7 capsule, becoming the first wrist chronograph to travel into space. The model had become a milestone in the history of watchmaking.

For its ubiquity in the aeronautical world, the first Navitimer's Breitling emblem bore the initials AOPA inside it, for the Aircraft Owners and Pilots Association.

THE 1950s —

1952

1952

Constellation
Omega   1952

Exciting scientific research conducted in the 1950s led to a deeper knowledge of the universe and would allow for the first explorations of the cosmos.

Omega's designers dedicated themselves to the production of a model whose name and appearance could embody the rigour of astronomical research as well as the precision of their chronometers, as verified by the Geneva Observatory. Their dedicated work led to the 1952 launch of the first line of self-winding wrist chronometers with the name Constellation, in homage to the stars and their splendour. The model met with immediate success, as an ideal synthesis of design and cutting-edge technology. The eight stars on its medallion represent the eight precision records the brand set at the Kew-Teddington and Geneva observatories in the mid-twentieth century. In 1982 a new version of the Constellation was launched, which was more impermeable due to four gold claws clamping either side of the dial. The Roman numerals on the bezel, further emphasised by the claws, soon became the distinctive symbol of the Constellation model.

Over the years, the watches in this line (one of the *maison*'s successes) have included models designed for women, jewelled variants, and a version displaying both the weekday and date with just a click.

Gold watch with round case, dial with 12 indices, and a star symbolising the collection, indices in beaten and polished gold, dauphine hands in polished gold, reinforced crystal and steel case, water-resistant down to 30 metres (approx. 100 feet).

Fifty Fathoms
Blancpain   1953

In the early 1950s, Jean-Jacques Fiechter was a pioneer in sports diving watches. Thanks to his diving experiences, he knew that divers' lives depended on their watches' reliability, and at that time there were no suitable watches. As the CEO of Blancpain, he mobilised his teams of horologists to meet the challenges posed to time measurement in an underwater environment. He drew up a detailed list of requirements for what would become the first mechanical diving watch: water-resistant and automatic with excellent legibility, even in difficult conditions. A series of solutions were patented in order to achieve these characteristics: a double-sealed system for the crown, which guaranteed water resistance even in the event of accidental extraction; a rotating bezel with indices to be used together with the minute hand to check elapsed time; and a locking mechanism to prevent the bezel from rotating during the dive. To solve the common issue of screw-in casebacks not sealing properly, a double O-ring seal was incorporated, overlapped by another metal disc to hold it in place.

Blancpain launched the Fifty Fathoms model in 1953. Its water resistance was guaranteed to over 90 metres (300 feet); a fathom is the unit of measurement of the marine arms in Great Britain and the United States, measuring about 1.8 metres (6 feet). At the time, this was considered the maximum depth that a diver could reach with the oxygen-air mixture that was available. This model also managed to satisfy the requests of a special unit of the French Navy: combat divers. Today Blancpain offers a range of watches that are water-resistant to a depth of 1,000 metres (about 3,300 feet), attesting to the maker's special relationship with the undersea world.

Dials are usually dark in colour to facilitate hand and index reading in less-than-optimal light conditions. Watch with 41mm/1⅗in-diameter steel case, black dial and rubber strap.

THE 1950s —

1953

— THE 1950s

Explorer
Rolex 1953

On 29 May 1953, at 11.30 in the morning, New Zealander Edmund Hillary and Nepalese Tenzing Norgay reached the highest point on Earth: the summit of Mt Everest at 8,484 metres (about 27,800 feet). The two remained on the summit for only fifteen minutes before they descended and rejoined the members of their party. They were not the first to try, but thus far the mountain had sent back many great expeditions and solo attempts. The undertaking, which would be difficult even today, was truly extraordinary at the time, considering the equipment and tools that were available. Oxygen supply was especially important, not only for climbing, but for the climbers' very survival. It was therefore essential to monitor the consumption of stocks by precisely and carefully keeping track of time.

Rolex supplied a shipment of watches made especially for the occasion, equipped with an Oyster case, a Perpetual movement, and a leather strap. These were the prototype of a model later to be called the Explorer. For Rolex, the Everest ascent presented an excellent opportunity to test their watches in extreme conditions (sudden changes in temperature and pressure at high altitudes), but it also constituted an important promotional launch. That same year, the company registered the Explorer trademark and began to market the model.

The wristwatch worn by Hillary and Norgay would in fact be produced in multiple editions – with a black dial; an oversized arrow index at 12 o'clock; and Arabic numerals at 3, 6 and 9 o'clock. All were made under the Explorer name.

The Explorer II, which had a date display, was introduced in 1971. It differed from the original for its additional orange 24-hour hand and fixed 24-hour graduated bezel, guaranteeing a differentiation between day and night-time hours.

Watch with a 36mm (1⅜in) case, steel bracelet, and black dial, with a large arrow index at 12 o'clock and Arabic numerals at 3, 6 and 9 o'clock. Without lighting, the watch continues to be legible, thanks to the luminescent substance applied to its indices and hands.

Submariner
Rolex 1953

What did Sean Connery, playing the world's most famous secret agent in 1964's *Goldfinger*, and the Cuban political leader Ernesto "Che" Guevara have in common? A Rolex Submariner. Images of both men are iconic: the former wears an impeccable tuxedo with a white jacket and consults his watch before heading into action; the second lights a cigar, displaying the timepiece he wears on his wrist. Credit for having contributed to making the Submariner watch a success, however, goes to the actor.

First marketed in 1954, the Oyster Perpetual Submariner, water-resistant for up to 100 metres (about 330 feet), was born of a technical innovation that allowed divers to measure the time spent underwater. This was thanks to its rotating bezel, designed to turn only anticlockwise, so mistakes could not be made when setting the time measurement. It was a fundamental innovation and would soon be adopted by other makers as well. Yet the way Connery turned this "technical" watch into a luxury item was something completely new, wearing it in action sequences or while sporting a tuxedo, and always doing so with great style.

Since it was first made in 1953, the Submariner has been continuously evolving, with enhancements in water resistance, robustness and functionality. In 1959, the crown's protective shoulders were introduced. Minute markers were added to the first quarter of an hour on its bezel. The bezel itself had pronounced grooves, making it easier to grip, even while wearing diving gloves. Its water resistance was improved, guaranteed for depths up to 300 metres (about 1,000 feet) for the Submariner Date in 1979 and for the Submariner in 1989. In 2008 and 2012, respectively, each model was enhanced with a new rotating bezel with a Cerachrom disc, with gold or platinum markers.

The first editions of the Submariner (references 6204 and 6205) bore a black dial; dot, baton and dagger hour markers; gold graphics; "pencil" hands; and a convex crystal and caseback, with no date aperture. Meanwhile, its signature unidirectional rotating bezel, also black, is engraved with 60 minute markers, alternating between Arabic numerals and bar indices. The water resistance of the 38mm (1½in) case was guaranteed down to 100 metres (approx. 330 feet).

THE 1950s —

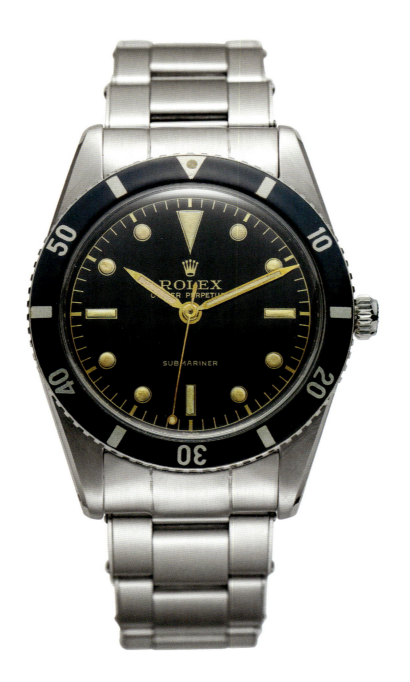

1953

— THE 1950s

1954

Type XX
Breguet 1954

The Breguet family's links to aviation date back to the early twentieth century. In 1907, Louis Charles Breguet, great-grandson of the famous watchmaker, and his brother Jacques devised a prototype for a vehicle that could take off vertically – a helicopter. In 1919, alongside another partner, Louis Charles founded the airline Compagnie des messageries aériennes (CMA), which would eventually become part of Air France.

In 1918, the Breguet *maison* began to produce watches for aviators, and then moved on to the manufacture of the chronograph mechanisms installed in aircraft dashboards. Already a supplier to the French Navy, the maker's ties to the military were drawn closer when the need to form a Naval Air Force became evident, shortly following the appearance of the first aeroplanes.

In 1954, the French Air Force commissioned the watchmaker to create a chronograph for aviators that would be called "Cronographe Type XX". This watch, based on standards issued by the Air Force in the 1950s, was designed to respond to pilots' needs during blind flight, for approach procedures, and for checking navigation and fuel consumption.

The Type XX was one of the first watches to have a flyback function which allowed the chronograph to be reset by simply pressing the push-piece at the bottom, thus considerably speeding up pilots' timing procedures during flight.

Watch with round 38mm (1½in) steel case; black dial; luminous Arabic numerals, and large luminous hands; an oversized crown for easy winding with gloves; a flyback function allowing the pilot to stop, reset and restart the chronograph via a single press of the lower push-piece.

Ingenieur
IWC Schaffhausen 1955

The Ingenieur originated with an ambitious project: to build a perfectly protected, ultra-precise watch that could be wound with just a movement of the wrist. This goal was achieved with the first pawl-winding system by Albert Pellaton, patented in the early 1950s. To deflect magnetic fields surrounding the watch, a technique from the construction of the Mark 11 pilot's watch was used, enclosing the automatic movement in an additional soft-iron inner case, with a dial in the same material.

In 1976, the aesthetic of the watch was revised by designer Gérald Genta, who decided to make the screws used to seal the case visible, displaying them on the bezel. That year saw the creation of the Ingenieur SL.

When IWC began to construct cases from titanium in the early 1980s, the ultra-thin Ingenieur Titan, reference 3350, was a pioneering model in using the revolutionary material. Finally, in 1989 with the reference 3508, IWC presented an Ingenieur that, with antimagnetic protection of up to 500,000 A/m (amperes per metre), could even withstand a magnetic resonance scanner. The Big Ingenieur, with a 45.5mm ($1^4/_5$ in) steel case, enjoyed considerable success in 2007 and was joined the following year by versions in platinum and rose gold.

Today, the Ingenieur range is synonymous with functional, resistant timepieces, perfectly equipped to handle water, shocks, vibrations and sudden changes in temperature.

Watch with 37mm (1½ in) steel case, silver soleil dial, luminous pencil hands and stick indices, central seconds, date aperture at 3 o'clock, and a leather strap.

THE 1950s —

1955

— THE 1950s

1955

GMT-Master
Rolex 1955

In the 1950s, commercial airlines made global exploration more accessible than it had ever been before. This created a significant challenge for pilots, whose work was based on accuracy. In search of a timepiece that could better serve the pilots in its fleet, Pan Am Airlines, the first airline to operate non-stop intercontinental flights, approached Rolex and asked them to create a watch that could simultaneously display the local time at the destination and place of departure. This is how the GMT-Master was born, introduced in 1955. It allowed for the display of a second time zone with the inclusion of a fourth, 24-hour hand in addition to the standard hour, minute and seconds hands.

The technical solution was rendered all the more effective by the GMT-Master's characteristic two-tone rotating bezel with numerals marking the 24 hours. The two colours of the bezel corresponded to daytime (red) or night-time (blue); this simple additional feature made the job of quickly determining the time in a foreign location even easier.

Although the GMT-Master had been created for professional pilots, it soon became a favourite watch among the nascent class of frequent flyers and jet-setters, who could afford not only travel, but luxury travel. In 1983, Rolex created the GMT-Master II, allowing for the time in two different time zones to be read simultaneously: the local time and a reference time, or the local time and that of another time zone. The date is synchronised with the local time display.

The blue-and-red bezel of the original has been nicknamed "Pepsi" among collectors. Later variations include the red-and-black "Coke", brown-and-gold "Root Beer" and blue-and-black "Batman". More recently, the aluminium bezel inlay has been replaced with ceramic, while still keeping many of the iconic colour combinations.

Speedmaster
Omega 1957

Introduced in the late 1950s, the Speedmaster chronograph would become famous for accompanying all space missions from the 1960s onward.

The very first models, with the reference number 2915, are considered the rarest and most collectible "Speedy" watches: a Speedmaster with reference number 2915-1 was sold for a record price of 3,115,500 Swiss francs in 2021 (over US$3.4 million/£2.7 million at the time). This first generation has two specific hallmarks: an engraved stainless-steel bezel (later models would have black bezels for improved visibility), and a "broad arrow" hour hand.

Omega conceived the Speedmaster as a racing watch. Created for professional racing-car drivers, it was perfectly legible and easy to use, and it was also the first watch in the world to feature a tachymeter scale on the bezel instead of on the dial. This feature was ideal for timing the average speed of laps on the track and complemented its robust design. The timepiece was extremely precise and water-resistant. The advertising campaign for its launch touted the watch as a "high-precision wrist computer" designed for "men who reckon the time in seconds." The Speedmaster wasn't just for racers, but for anyone who lived life at a fast pace.

It was the generation that followed, the reference CK2998, that brought the Speedmaster to "cosmic" fame. American astronaut Walter Schirra wore his personal Speedmaster during the Mercury-Atlas 8 flight mission on 3 October 1962, becoming the first man in space with an Omega on his wrist. The Speedmaster was on the astronauts' wrists during the July 1969 moon landing; it was the first and only watch to be worn on the moon.

Watch with a 39mm (1½in) case and steel bracelet: matt black dial with orange indices and luminous arrow hands; chronograph dials in the centre; bezel with tachymeter scale.

THE 1950s —

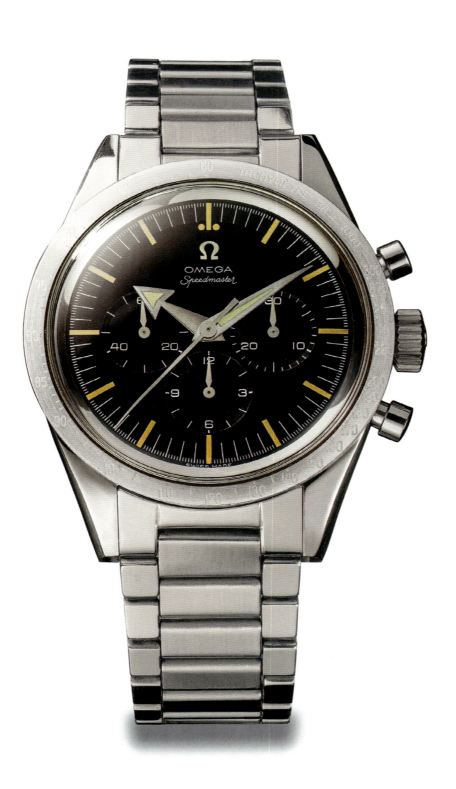

1957

— THE 1950s

1959

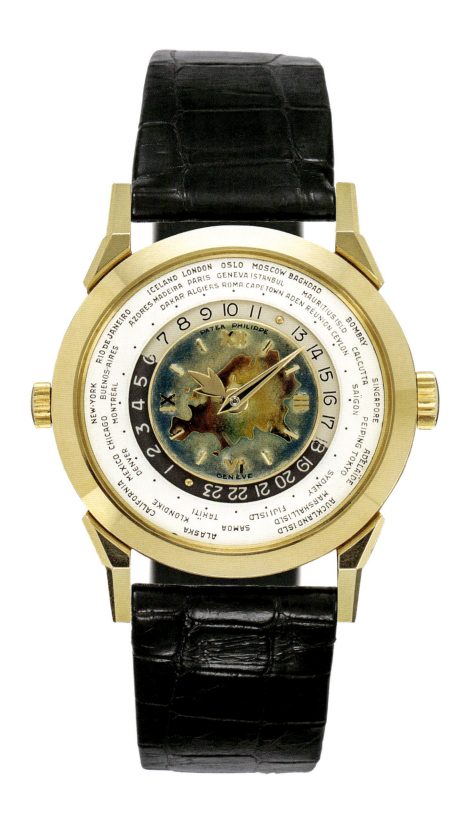

World Time
Patek Philippe 1959

Developed by Louis Cottier in the 1930s and already used by the watchmaker in a series of timepieces, Patek Philippe's ingenious world-time complication was patented by the maker in 1959. Patek Philippe world-time watches traditionally feature a dial with a guilloché pattern at the centre or a polychrome decoration in cloisonné enamel. The cloisonné decoration is a highly sought-after detail in auction sales, always representing just a portion of a given hemisphere. Thanks to its two rotating discs at the periphery of the dial, the time in all 24 time zones can be read at a single glance. Its division of the world into 24 time zones, each covering approximately fifteen degrees of longitude, was adopted at the International Meridian Conference (1884) and has undergone only slight changes since. The external (location) disc bears the names of 24 cities, each representing a time zone, while the internal (24-hour) disc displays the hours corresponding to each of these time zones. On a Patek Philippe world-time watch, the local time marked by the hands corresponds to that of the selected time zone at 12 o'clock. On the right are time zones east of this location, and on the left are those west of it. The position of the minute hand remains the same. This technical achievement would take another step forwards in 1999: a new mechanism made it possible to change the time-zone indication with the single press of a button, all without altering the precision of the movement by a single second.

Gold wristwatch with heures universelles *(world time) complication and enamelled dial depicting Eurasia.*

The 1960s

Pop Revolution

The 1960s brought on significant societal changes. The reopening of markets, expansive force of capitalism, and renewed international monetary stability allowed the most advanced economies to develop at a sustained pace. Overall, living conditions improved in the most industrialised countries, and ever-larger sectors of their populations were able to access consumer goods. The sociopolitical and cultural events of these years would inevitably influence and profoundly alter the values, aspirations and lifestyles of generations to follow.

The 1960s were the years of The Beatles, of coloured plastics, fluorescent lighting, and ready-to-wear clothing. Product design was characterised by a strong tendency towards abstraction as well as rounded shapes helping to generate a feeling of comfort and wellbeing, in some ways resembling atmospheres of an almost futuristic character. Fabrics and surfaces boasted waves of colour in the most brilliant and intense shades, as well as optical motifs, featuring original, cheerful lines and geometric shapes.

The "Pop" Art of Andy Warhol and Roy Lichtenstein portrayed objects from everyday life that had taken on value in consumer society; these included economy cars, refrigerators, washing machines, tinned food, detergents and packaged drinks. This art spoke a language known to everyone – that of mass media, advertising, television and cinema – which increasingly influenced people's choices.

In this context, the relationship between movies and fashion grew stronger. Motion pictures especially contributed to the fame of select watch models. This includes examples featured in the James Bond series, like the Rolex Submariner worn by Sean Connery from 1962 to 1967, the GMT-Master sported by Honor

◀ *Beatles drummer Ringo Starr in a photograph from the 1960s.*

Blackman as Pussy Galore in *Goldfinger*, and a Breitling Navitimer in *Thunderball*; in this last, the watch belongs to French Air Force pilot François Derval and is recovered by Bond in the finale to be returned to Bond's co-lead, the pilot's daughter. In the 1968 film *The Thomas Crown Affair*, a Cartier Tank Cintrée and a Memovox by Jaeger-LeCoultre were both worn by Steve McQueen. McQueen stepped out of his typical tough-character roles to play the well-dressed, refined Thomas Crown, and the two elegant watches helped to complete his new look.

The Peacock Revolution

If men's fashion in previous decades had undergone little change, the developments that occurred in the sixties were extraordinary. Music and the artistic image had a strong cultural influence, and this included the world of fashion, where clothing progressively became more colourful, unisex, and inspired by Asian cultures.

Formal clothing from the early part of the decade emphasised slimming lines. Jackets were mostly single-breasted with side vents and paired with straight-legged trousers. Mid-eveningwear featured the broken suit, consisting of a jacket in a solid, darker colour than one's trousers. For evening dress, the tuxedo's shawl collar was replaced with a single breasted jacket design with slim lapels. Over the course of the decade, however, men's clothing would integrate elements that had traditionally been considered feminine, like shirts enhanced with ruffles and lace, short, slim sweaters fitted at the waist, belts with flashy buckles, and tight, low-waisted trousers in bright colours.

Towards the middle of the decade, however, what is known as the "peacock revolution" took place. Hippie culture propagated the influence of ethnic themes, especially those linked to cultures in the Far East, with bright colours, psychedelic patterns, or paisley prints inspired by Indian clothing, including collarless jackets. This fashion mixed Eastern styles with military wear, popularised on the album cover of The Beatles' *Sgt. Pepper's Lonely Hearts Club Band* (1967), where the famous Liverpool group is shown wearing contrasting, vividly coloured reinterpretations of military uniforms. Even the most traditionalist men's fashion was influenced by a preference for certain Asian motifs, manifesting itself not only in clothing, but also in the adoption of brightly coloured decorations and patterns.

Space, the future, and dreams were other main themes of the decade. Pierre Cardin was designing futuristic suits for men. One need only consider his 1966/67 "Cosmos" collection, which included elements like turtleneck sweaters and zip-up tunics in jersey, new both in terms of style and materials, or the geometries of Paco Rabanne's garments, which revolutionised fashion by introducing a lunar, science-fiction style, influenced by the 1969 moon landing. The fashion industry was adopting modern designs to create a more liberating, playful look.

Stone Dials

The restless, provocative 1960s was a period of a great revolution in dress throughout the Western world. Fashion, refusing all previous

THE 1960s

Piaget, automatic watch with bracelet, white gold and cushion shaped with jade dial, c. 1965.

canons, was filled with colour, establishing links with the world of art and design. It would also continue to define new horizons of luxury, experimenting with new shapes and materials.

In the watchmaking sector, Piaget interpreted the spirit of the time through the introduction of a completely innovative aesthetic. The ultra-flat calibre produced by the *maison* provided a technical basis for experimenting with form and design. The mechanical Calibre 9P from 1956, which was 2 millimetres ($^7/_{100}$ inch) thick, and the 2.3-millimetre-thick ($^9/_{100}$-inch-thick) automatic 12P movement from 1960 made it possible to alter wristwatch design by widening the dial, therefore improving its legibility without increasing the thickness of the watch. Piaget's slogan, "the watch of the international elite" appeared in the maker's catalogue in 1957. In 1964, it presented its first watches with dials created entirely of precious stones: lapis lazuli, onyx, turquoise and tiger's eye, as well as coral and malachite, at times combined in a highly imaginative manner with brushed gold and diamonds. The stone dials generally had polished surfaces, but there were versions available with a matt finish or engraved with delicate designs.

CLASSIC LINES AND REBELLIOUS SHAPES

Patek Philippe's work in the field of design led to the development of the Golden Ellipse, a watch model introduced in 1968 inspired by the golden ratio (1.618 to 1). Discovered by ancient Greek mathematicians, this relationship has been used since then as a basis for great architectural and artistic works, establishing the perfect point at which a line is to be divided into two harmonious but unequal segments. The Golden Ellipse presented a new aesthetic that was simple, yet daring. Being a gold watch with a gold dial (albeit lacquered in cobalt blue), it reasserted the concept of luxury. Noted for its precious materials and colours, the watch was destined to become one of the maker's classics.

The aesthetics of the 1960s were innovative, creative – even rebellious, and the paradigms of a new, unconventional perspective were also to be found in the build of certain watches.

During the sixties, Patek Philippe collaborated with the designer Gilbert Albert to give life to the "Asymmetric" collection. Albert joined

— THE 1960s

In Patek Philippe's "Asymmetric" collection, watch models' shapes are deconstructed and their angles asymmetrical, but the final result is always in perfect balance.

the *maison* in 1955 and remained there for seven years as *chef d'atelier*. His creativity gave birth to the most daring models of the time, paying tribute to modern sculpture, especially to the Romanian sculptor Constantin Brâncuși and the Dutch painter Piet Mondrian.

In the area of complications, Patek Philippe introduced the reference 3448 in 1962, a watch with a perpetual calendar, animated by an automatic movement. Its crisp, linear design moved away from the classic rounded shapes of the bezels and lugs typifying previous models. In these years, Audemars Piguet also ventured into creating timepieces of daring asymmetry.

In 1967, the Cartier Crash was born, with an unusual genesis and unmistakable shape.

Initial Setbacks

Introduced in 1963, a hand-wound chronograph was born as simply the "Rolex Cosmograph" ("Daytona" only being added to the name at a later date), and it received a rather cold reception. At the time, classic and ultra-flat watches were more in vogue: such a modern, sporty model did not accord with contemporary tastes, which preferred ultra-thin watches with less rigid shapes. On the other hand, the watch was designed so professional racing-car drivers could measure their times, displaying them on the dial in the form of hours, minutes and seconds. At first, the Daytona was not particularly successful on the market. As a consequence, Rolex experimented, gradually introducing various small changes: dials of different colours, positioning text in different locations, and indices of various kinds. Each edition was

Audemars Piguet asymmetrical watch, yellow gold case, off-centre silver-plated dial, central hour and minute indication.

introduced in extremely limited quantities. Today, these ultra-rare models are some of the most valuable and desirable watches on the collectors' market. One of the most famous Daytona models was called the Paul Newman. The actor had received it as a gift from his wife, and he wore it while filming a movie set in the world of motor racing. Models named after the famous actor can be identified by the unique graphics of the dial: it has contrasting counters, with the background colour of the continuous seconds scale also matching that of the internal counters.

Watch on the Moon

In this era of great prosperity, one event attracted the attention of the entire world: mankind's extraordinary venture into space. A dream that had been pursued for centuries became a reality, as if by magic, with the event amplified by live images, keeping hundreds of millions of people fixed to their television screens.

It was 20 July 1969. Richard Nixon, president of the United States, would declare "This is the greatest week in the history of the world since Creation." When astronaut Neil Armstrong landed on the moon, he was accompanied on the surface by Buzz Aldrin and, in orbit around the moon, Michael Collins.

On each of their wrists was an Omega Speedmaster watch, which would become the official watch of subsequent NASA missions.

In the quest to conquer space, a Breitling Navitimer chronograph was the first "wrist instrument" to orbit the Earth when, on 24 May

Omega's Speedmaster was selected for manned space missions from 1965. When NASA astronauts were engaged in extravehicular activities, they wore the Speedmaster, fixed securely and in a way that was easily legible while wearing their spacesuits.

1962, Scott Carpenter completed three orbits around the Earth aboard the Aurora 7 spacecraft wearing this model.

The fate of the Speedmaster, however, already seemed to be sealed with the Mercury flight of 3 October 1962, in which astronaut Walter Schirra wore his own personal Omega on his wrist.

The timepiece would feature prominently in other important stories related to man's conquest of space. It was on a Speedmaster that Commander Jim Lovell, having uttered the famous phrase "Houston, we have a problem", measured the critical 14 seconds marking the entry of Apollo 13 into the Earth's atmosphere in 1970. The secret behind the authority of the watch is its mechanism's robustness and the components used in the production of its case. An example of the latter is its extremely resistant hesalite crystal, which, in the case of breakage in the spacecraft's cabin, will not shatter into a thousand pieces; it thus prevents tiny fragments from being dispersed in the air, a condition that could present a serious safety risk in zero gravity. The manual-winding Speedmaster Professional is the only model suitable for use in space, as the vacuum would not guarantee the optimal functioning of an automatic movement's rotor: this is the reason that it is still enabled by NASA for extravehicular activities and that it has also been chosen by the Russian space agency.

Technical Innovations

In its work to make automatic watches in the 1960s, Girard-Perregaux made an important contribution to the development of precision movements. In 1957, the maker had introduced a winding system called the Gyromatic, which improved the performance of the winding rotor. In 1965, it instead launched a high-frequency movement, which oscillated at 36,000 beats per hour and was destined to significantly improve performance in terms of precision.

In 1969, Zenith introduced a high-frequency automatic chronograph powered by a new generation of calibre. While other balance wheels generally oscillate at a rate of eight beats per second, the El Primero calibre does so at ten per second. The mechanism debuted with three different steel models, one of which was the A385, a tonneau-shaped steel chronograph with a brown gradient dial. A year later, the watch was chosen for Zenith's "Operation Sky", an extreme test in which the chronograph was fixed to the landing gear of an Air France Boeing 707 during a flight from Paris to New York. This was to verify the timepiece's resistance to harsh atmospheric conditions over the course of the trip, such as drastic changes in temperature and atmospheric pressure, as well as wind strength. Upon the 707's landing, the watch still worked perfectly.

Underwater Precision

Fascination for the underwater world spurred an unprecedented effort to systematically explore new depths. The watch industry was tasked with developing waterproof, robust and, above all, reliable diving watches. Divers' health, and even their lives, depended on the precise management of immersion times. In 1967, with the growing popularity of water

— THE 1960s

sports and a passion for diving, IWC developed the first Aquatimer, water-resistant up to 20 bar (1 bar is approximately 1 atmospheric pressure at sea level) and equipped with an internal rotating bezel for displaying dive times. The watch was the beginning of IWC's success in the realm of diving watches.

Also in 1967, the Sea-Dweller was born from a collaboration between Rolex and Comex (Compagnie maritime d'expertises), a French company specialising in submarine engineering.

Initially, the French company's divers used the Submariner, which was water-resistant to

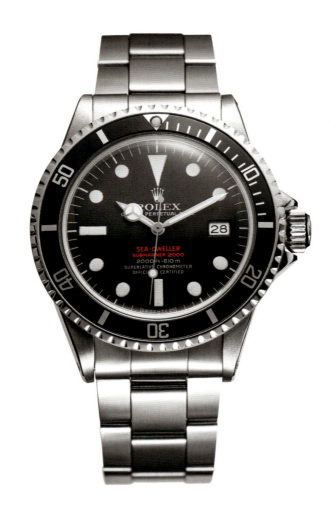

The Rolex Sea-Dweller was created in 1967 to meet the needs of divers.

Jaeger-LeCoultre's Memovox Polaris featured a black dial with a three-ring concentric layout, a rotating inner bezel, and a double crown case. Signatures of the design were the model's elongated Arabic numerals and the trapezoidal hour markers and baton hands, covered with a cream-coloured luminescent coating.

The 42mm (1 7⁄10in) steel case featured three prominent crowns: one to adjust the time, the second to control the rotating bezel, and the third for additional functions, like the Memovox.

200 metres (656 feet); but the helium used in the hyperbaric (decompression) chambers, which penetrated the watch, risked creating such pressure that it would shatter its crystal. So the *maison* prepared a solution suited to their specific needs.

To solve the problem, Rolex patented a one-way valve allowing gas to escape, which enabled

THE 1960s

Bulova's Accutron watch, introduced in 1960, was one of the first watch models to use a tuning fork. The skeletonised model allows its mechanism to remain visible.

This system, patented by Rolex, allows the watch to withstand the colossal pressure present at 3,900 metres (12,795 feet), which is equivalent to placing the weight of about three tonnes (tons) on the watch.

In 1965, Jaeger-LeCoultre introduced the Memovox Polaris, a diving watch with a large case and an alarm function.

CHANGES IN THE MARKET

In 1957, the American manufacturer Hamilton announced the Electric 500 to the press: it was the first electric watch, the beginning of a technological revolution that would change the watch industry forever. The success of the Hamilton Electric was short-lived. In 1960, the Bulova family introduced the Accutron, the first watch to use a tuning fork as a regulating organ, replacing what is known as a balance wheel or pendulum in mechanical watches.

The movement of the tuning fork, the watchmaker's crowning achievement, guaranteed a maximum deviation of one minute per month. The name "Accutron" is formed from the words "accuracy" and "electronic".

In 1969, Seiko introduced the Astron model, a wristwatch with a quartz movement of very small dimensions. It was the beginning of the quartz era. Thinner, more precise, more modern, and more suited to the fashion of the time than traditional timepieces, quartz watches would throw the mechanical watch industry into crisis.

the helium accumulated in the watch to be released at a specific pressure during the decompression phase, while maintaining the Oyster case's impermeability.

This innovation has perfected the internal and external pressure resistance of the Sea-Dweller's case, making it a perfectly suited watch to meet the needs of professional divers. The Rolex Deepsea owes its exceptional characteristics of strength, water resistance, and pressure resistance to its Ringlock system.

1963

Daytona
Rolex 1963

Launched in 1963, the Cosmograph Daytona was designed to meet professional racing-car drivers' chronometric needs. This chronograph allows drivers to measure their times, displayed on the dial in the form of hours, minutes and seconds. The hours and minutes are read on the characteristic counters, at 9 and 3 o'clock respectively, while the seconds are displayed on the 60-second scale that surrounds the dial and are indicated by the central, arrow-tipped hand. The bezel features a tachymeter scale that allows the wearer to read the average speed over a given distance based on the time measured. The first models were equipped with chronograph pump pushers. These were then substituted in 1965 for screw-in push-pieces for greater water resistance in the reference 6240. Today, the Daytona's chronograph function is still activated by push-pieces which, like the winding crown, screw in when not in use. Rolex master watchmakers have perfected the mechanism to adapt it to the optimal pressure of a finger on the buttons and for the chronograph to activate instantly. The Cosmograph Daytona pays homage to Daytona, Florida, birthplace of the passion for speed and racing in the early twentieth century. The name tells of the historical, privileged link that unites Rolex with motor racing.

In 1988, Rolex introduced the self-winding Cosmograph Daytona using the Zenith El Primero movement, the Daytona reference 16520. In 2000, Rolex presented the new Daytona model, reference 116520, which is fully manufactured by Rolex, including its mechanism.

Reference 6239 was the first Daytona model launched by Rolex.
　Watch with 40mm (1⅜in) case and steel bracelet, black dial with white chronograph counters, and a tachymeter scale on the bezel.
　With its tachymeter scale, three counters, and push-piece buttons, the Cosmograph Daytona was created to be the best timekeeping tool for racing-car drivers.

Crash
Cartier   1967

While the design of the Crash does have a certain formal affinity with the clocks depicted by Salvador Dalí in his painting *The Persistence of Memory*, there is no concrete evidence of a link between this timepiece and the work of the surrealist painter. The story is that the idea for the Crash was born in 1967, when a customer took his Bagnoire, which was misshapen following a car accident, to be repaired at Cartier's London branch. The broken watch gave Jean-Jacques Cartier, then owner of the firm, the idea to produce an altogether new and unusual asymmetric shape. The very name "crash" appears to support this claim.

Over the years, the *maison* has always experimented with geometry, favouring, in turn, the square, the rectangle, the tonneau, or the oval to a more circular shape. The asymmetrical Crash, however, was born during a period of vast creativity: the 1960s, a time of irreverence, irony and unconventionality.

However, even if its design did emerge during this time, its shape differed significantly from all other watches created in the same period. Perhaps this is precisely where its charm lies: its abstract character is in a sense transcendent, and therefore timeless – so much so that the Crash has over time attracted various collectors, including creators like the celebrated hip-hop artist and producer Kanye West.

Crash wristwatch, Cartier London, 1967. Yellow gold, pink gold, one sapphire cabochon, leather strap.

Barrel-shaped LeCoultre Calibre 840 movement, Côtes de Genève decoration, rhodium-plated, 17 jewels, shock-resistant, Swiss lever escapement, monometallic balance, flat balance spring.

Tradition holds that this model represents an interpretation of a watch damaged in a crash. Cartier Collection.

THE 1960s —

1967

— THE 1960s

1967

Aquatimer
IWC Schaffhausen 1967

In 1967, with the growing popularity of sport diving, IWC developed the Aquatimer model. The case was waterproof to a depth of 200 metres (656 feet), while the rotating bezel for setting the dive time was installed beneath the glass to prevent movement while diving.

In 1968, versions were produced with coloured dials; in addition to black, they were available in red and blue, and their water resistance was increased to 300 metres (984 feet).

The collaboration between the designer F.A. Porsche and IWC between 1978 and 1998 led to a revolutionary material being used for watches: titanium. In 1982, the Porsche Design Ocean 2000 was born; with its structure and use of titanium alloys, one could reach a depth of 2,000 metres (6,560 feet).

In 1988, IWC created an antimagnetic timepiece for mine-clearance divers. To keep the mine from exploding prematurely, it was essential that the magnetic field generated by the watch be minimal. For this reason, the model was equipped with a movement in non-magnetisable material, the IWC Calibre 3755AM, also known as the 3755 Amag calibre.

The GST Deep One was revealed in 1999, the first IWC watch model with a mechanical depth gauge that informed the diver of their current depth.

In 2004, IWC created a radically innovative movement: the Aquatimer Minute Memory. Thanks to the patented split-seconds hand, the dive time was indicated three times: on the internal bezel; with the chronograph; and by means of the split-seconds hand, which especially helped in determining the time already elapsed during a dive.

Watch with 40mm (1½in) steel case, black dial, luminescent indices and baton hands, black leather bracelet.

Golden Ellipse
Patek Philippe 1968

Launched for the first time in 1968, the Golden Ellipse sought to represent the principle of the golden ratio applied to watchmaking. It is this relationship, formulated by ancient Greek mathematicians, which determines the perfect point at which to divide a line into two harmonious but unequal segments, the "divine proportion" (approximately 1.618 to 1) on which great architectural and artistic works are based. The Golden Ellipse offered a new, simple, but daring aesthetic that reaffirmed the concept of luxury, a gold watch with a gold dial, but lacquered in cobalt blue. Shortly after it was launched, the first variations appeared in yellow gold and then in white, with a gold bracelet in a woven pattern, dials with solely Roman numerals or dials with Roman numerals and baton indices, rounded and embossed bezels, and even with the dial rotated by 90 degrees.

In addition to the original version in yellow gold with a metallic blue gold dial, the maker has recently revisited this classic by offering rose- and white-gold versions combined with dials of various tones.

The original large Golden Ellipse, highly esteemed by collectors, was produced from the late sixties into the early eighties.

With the reference 5378, created in 2008 to celebrate the model's fortieth anniversary, Patek Philippe introduced a large edition with a platinum case.

Watch with 34mm (1⅓in) case and blue alligator, cobalt-blue gold dial, applied gold indices and baton hands.

THE 1960s —

1968

— THE 1960s

1969

El Primero
Zenith 1969

In 1969, the same year that the Concorde took flight and the first man set foot on the moon, Zenith introduced an integrated automatic chronograph with a column wheel, the El Primero calibre, distinguished by the frequency of its balance wheel: while other balance wheels generally oscillate at a rate of 8 beats per second, the El Primero calibre does so at a rate of 10. The development of this movement was accompanied by numerous incredible innovations, including a dry lubricant guaranteeing extraordinary long-term stability; and also its power reserve of approximately fifty hours, optimised to cope with higher and more frequent energy consumption. Its absolute precision allowed it to pass COSC tests (by the Contrôle officiel suisse des chronomètres) and be certified a fully fledged chronometer. The El Primero calibre was used in a number of references, including the A386 in steel, as well as the G381 and G582 in gold. Reference A386, destined to become the reference model of the Chronomaster line, was launched in 1969; it had a round case with straight lugs, as well as decimal and tachymeter scales.

The hallmark of the El Primero model was the multicoloured dial with three differently coloured counters and a red chronograph hand for better legibility.

The Chronomaster El Primero, featuring a 38mm (1½in) steel case with a brown alligator strap, has a silvered dial and iconic chronograph counters.

The 1970s

The Formidable 1970s

Eclectic, memorable and revolutionary both socially and culturally, the 1970s brought about great changes in the aesthetic field, as they did elsewhere. Bright yet warm colours, geometric macro patterns, and glossy surfaces defined the design products of the time, which were billed as "anti-classic" and stood out for their unusual style.

The decade was characterised by a yearning for freedom that expressed itself through various forms of transgression, political and social struggles, and, above all, by a great creative ferment in all sectors. These were the years of youth protest and flower children, of pop and rock music, and of cultural, social and political enterprise. They were years of intellectual investment, reflected not only in a certain segment of abstract or conceptual figurative art, with its technical experimentation (mixing acrylics, tempera, photographic images and various media, from cardboard to fabric, from metal to plastic), but also objects for everyday living whose aim was both aesthetic enjoyment and the development of thought as an activity.

In these same years, technology made great strides, laying the foundations for an information revolution that would be passed down to the present day. In 1971, Intel developed the first microprocessor; in 1977 came the Commodore PET, one of the first successful personal computers.

The transformation also affected the audiovisual sector, with the introduction of the first video recorders and video cassettes. Colour TV spread globally, and private cable television sets were born.

Thanks to the birth of new media, communication and marketing techniques were refined based on the concept of the image. Companies

◀ *Actor Steve McQueen was an icon of a rebellious, unconventional style.*

viewed integrated communication, or the wise use of marketing and media, as the best solution to market competition.

Differing Souls

Controversial and difficult, the 1970s were traversed by social tensions, as well as ideologies and a newfound freedom of body and mind. The decade had, in point of fact, in fashion as in many other areas, two souls: one nonconformist, the other elegant. These poles emerged particularly in the seventies' closing years. The concept of "personal taste" and free aesthetic choice developed in this time: fashion offered a mix of imaginative and eccentric styles, so all could express their personalities freely. Thus, alongside clothing selected to reflect one's political engagement, there was one object available that did not give up on classic chic.

The traditional suit continued to be a staple for many men, with slim single-breasted jackets, often with wide lapels and flared trousers. The shirts were often colourful, sometimes with floral prints, two-toned or with contrasting trims, had long collar points, and were perfectly suited to wearing with a waistcoat, which once again featured in the image of masculine elegance. These were form-fitting and worn closed in front. Sleeveless cardigans with striped or checkered designs replaced jackets in casual wear. For formal dress, tuxedos were also available in new materials like patterned velvet. Tuxedos were also established as a women's garment, thanks to Yves Saint Laurent, who put a women's tuxedo on the catwalk in 1975. In the late seventies, an androgynous style emerged that skillfully mixed masculine and feminine; the concept of unisex was born, with garments that could be worn by men and women alike: for instance, the Saharan jacket or fitted shirts and sweaters, worn by both sexes with silhouettes designed to slim all types.

The 1970s was a period of great originality in creative fields, and jewellery and watchmaking were also affected by the desire to experiment with new shapes, and often also new materials.

As the author has written elsewhere, "Among the jewels of the seventies were creations of mechanical inspiration as well: brooches and bracelets with geometric lines, according with a fashion that conveyed a masculine aesthetic. Jeweled accessories were often worn by men, from classic cufflinks to bracelets, rings, tie clips, brooches, tags, and pendants, as well as cigarette cases. Utility knives, money holders, and key rings also formed a part of a gentleman's clothing."[1]

Some makers chose a modern, linear style for their timepieces; they used oval or square-shaped cases but with softened corners, enriched and given added interest through workmanship. Dials were also gold or in contrasting colours, sometimes made of semi-precious stones or using coloured enamels and mother-of-pearl. Their surfaces were often engraved or given a matt "satin" finish. The surfaces of gold bracelets could be embossed and were also often satin-finished.

---

[1] Cappelletti, Mara, *Un quadrilatero d'oro*, in "Stile Milano – Storie di eleganza", Exhibition Catalogue, Nexo, Milan 2020, p. 38.

The High-Tech Revolution

As a result of in-depth research, the seventies saw the arrival of technological innovations that would influence the customs, the work and the very life of millions of people.

The year 1969 was an important one in the history of watchmaking. The Japanese company Seiko introduced the Astron model, the first wristwatch to use quartz technology. However, the Astron was still a model with an analogue dial. The first prototype of a digital watch had been presented by the American Hamilton Watch Co. three years earlier, with the name of Pulsar, and in 1972 the company put a model into production. This model, however, was limited by its high energy consumption. It was in 1973 that Seiko, having solved its technical challenges, shocked the world, launching the first quartz watch with a small liquid crystal display (LCD). On this watch, numbers could be read indicating the hours, minutes and seconds.

From then on, a trend for clocks with LCD displays exploded. Young people in particular abandoned classic watches with hands in favour of technological models. To these, companies gradually added functions apart from simply telling the time: stopwatch functions, alarms, and others. By the early eighties, they would also integrate certain calculation features into these watches. Casio, thanks to miniaturised integrated circuits, added highly specialised functions including depth gauges, altimeters, and blood pressure gauges. In 1976, Citizen began production of the Crystron Solar Cell, the first quartz watch whose battery was charged using sun exposure.

These watches were innovative not only from a technical standpoint, but also in terms of de-

Seiko's Astron model was the first quartz watch, introduced to the market in 1969.

sign: the material they used was steel for the case and bracelet, or synthetic materials for the strap. They also conveyed the unisex concept that was being expressed in fashion, to the degree that versions for "him" and for "her" differed only in size, not aesthetics.

The Japanese houses managed to conquer important market shares thanks to their watches' affordability, to the point of putting the traditional watch industry in crisis. Traditional horologists, however, had the courage to respond and found answers, both in terms of technology and marketing.

— THE 1970s

Swiss Quartz

At the beginning of the seventies, the large traditional watchmaking houses added a series of watches that used quartz movements to the production of their mechanical timepieces, to which they continued to dedicate their aesthetic and technical endeavours. To react to the advance of Japanese companies, Swiss *maisons* joined forces in a shared technological project. From this commitment was born the consortium called the CEH (Centre électronique horloger) which brought together all the great watchmaking houses, including Patek Philippe, Rolex, Piaget, IWC, Omega and Longines. At the Basel Fair in April 1970, the CEH presented the celebrated Beta-21 movement, which was used by watchmakers in the seventies, but always in combination with analogue dials. For example, Patek Philippe used it in its reference 3587 with a cushion case and woven bracelet in gold, and Rolex used it in its reference 5100 with Oyster case.

Later, makers began to develop quartz movements on their own. Rolex, for example, introduced the Oysterquartz in 1977, again with an Oyster case but with the Calibre 5035. The most classic reference is the 17000, made entirely of steel, which combined a smooth bezel with the integrated Oyster bracelet. An Oysterquartz would be on the wrist of the climber Reinhold Messner when he conquered Everest without supplemental oxygen in 1978.

Girard-Perregaux decided to tackle the advent of quartz by creating its own movements. These would become a point of reference for the market, and, between 1976 and 1978, the company produced the Casquette model with a digital display. In 1975, the *maison* introduced a model that

8,200 digital quartz models of Casquette by Girard-Perregaux were produced.

they named Laureato. Designed by the maker, the model stood out for its octagonal raised bezel and integrated bracelet. Inside ticked a slim, ultra-precise quartz movement, which in those years Girard-Perregaux had just presented for the first time.

The era of mechanical watchmaking then appeared to have come to an end; but precisely in this especially difficult, troubled period, Swiss companies decided to respond by changing their stance and adapting themselves in creative, daring ways to changes in taste, renewing traditional models in both design and concept.

Luxury Made of Steel

The international economic situation was not ideal, due to the oil crisis that had disturbed the market. On this premise, it was natural for the idea of luxury to change in favour of a new sobriety. It was in this context that an absolutely revolutionary idea was established: the luxury steel watch. The creative genius behind this concept was the designer Gérald Genta, who conveyed a very clear message: *haute horlogerie* could create prestigious models without necessarily relying on precious metals. It was the design, the precision of execution, and the quality of the movement that counted, no longer the materials used.

The figure of Genta is surrounded by legends regarding the genesis of the watches he designed. It is said that he only had one night to design the Royal Oak. In 1971, one day after the opening of the Swiss Watch Fair – an annual event in which all the most prestigious watchmakers present their new designs – Georges Golay, general manager of Audemars Piguet, phoned Genta asking him the impossible: to design a watch that had "never been seen before", to be presented to the brand's Italian distributor.

It typically takes several weeks and hundreds of designs to create a watch, and Genta was given only one night, but he persisted. That night, he designed not only the shape of the watch, but the dial, the indices, and the hands, as well – in short, every detail. His drawing would never be retouched. Up until then, mechanical watches had been made of gold, but Genta used steel: it was its captivating contours and the fine finishes that rendered the watch high-end. Its octagonal design, its sharp edges, and the visible screws on its bezel constituted a breaking point with the aesthetics of the time, which sought small dimensions and rounded shapes. Its market reception, at least at the beginning, was not enthusiastic.

In successive years, however, the model garnered appreciation, and subsequently its success was such that the watch became one of the maker's iconic models.

Sporting Elegance

Even Patek Philippe, a maker that produced mechanical watches of the highest calibre with refined complications, decided to offer a model designed by Genta, in order to appeal to an audience with different style needs. Inspired by the portholes of ocean liners, the watch is distinguished by a soft and sensual shape. The dial is embossed with a horizontal linear pattern, with baton indices and hands, and the date at 3 o'clock. Thus Patek Philippe presented a luxury sports watch, the Nautilus, in 1976.

Those managing the company understood that it was headed for many changes. A new kind of wealthy clientele was emerging, active both in work and in leisure time – successful men who took to the helm of their sailing yachts, skied down snow-covered slopes, or jogged at six in the morning to keep fit. This new generation had a penchant for challenge and enjoyed a dynamic lifestyle. Luxury watches in the 1970s, with easily scratched gold cases and the flattest possible profile, were mostly precious objects to wear in the evening on formal occasions. There was a need to design watches for dynamic managers who were at the office during the day, tennis at noon, and golf at weekends. The name of the watch refers to its water resistance even at great depths, an unusual feature for a Patek Philippe model. This design was also a success, one that has been passed down to the present

— THE 1970S

day. Reactions to the aesthetics of the Nautilus differed; some found it "shocking", while others were enthusiastic. It soon became clear that this watch was not intended for just anyone, but for a very specific clientele. During the 1980s, the number of these potential customers would grow significantly. The size of the watch (42 millimetres/1$^{7}/_{10}$ inches), criticised at the time of its launch, became one of its chief selling points.

SUCCESSFUL PROFESSIONALS

The Royal Oak and the Nautilus inaugurated the category of luxury sports watches, watches to be worn with tailor-made suits or with more casual clothing. Above all, they were marketed as a luxury item.

Other companies continued to update their professional watch offerings. This was the case with Rolex, which was able to maintain its competitive position even in this difficult period, thanks to the quality of its product and the company's meticulous, thorough sales and assistance services. In the 1970s, Rolex launched the Explorer II (1971) and the Sea-Dweller "4000" (1978), paving the way for its success to further develop.

Omega introduced the Ploprof, a professional diving watch that became a model of style with its clearly recognisable geometric shape. Gianni Agnelli, then president of Ferrari, sported a Ploprof over his shirt cuff, providing the watch with immediate visibility among the international jet set, and an appeal that far exceeded the professional sphere for which it was originally intended.

Patek Philippe introduced the reference 3587, animated by the Beta 21 movement, in 1969. It was available in yellow and white gold, with dials of different colours.

THE POWER OF THE LOGO

When, at the end of the seventies, the idea of brand recognition came to the fore, Bulgari began to use its brand in the decorative sphere, rendering the name of the fashion house a key element of its advertising campaigns, taking advantage of its repetition as a backdrop for jewellery, watches, and other products.

The year 1975 was a pivotal one for Bulgari's watchmaking sector: that year, the *maison* decided to donate a gold watch to its most loyal customers, designing a model with a glossy, wide bezel that bore an incised "Bulgari Rome" in two places instead of the house logo.

THE 1970s —

When you take your life in your hands, you need a good watch on your wrist.

When the divers of Operation Janus spent eight days working on the sea-bed below the Gulf of Ajaccio, they were all equipped with the same watch; the Omega Seamaster 600, our professional diver's watch. When Commander Cousteau needed a watch for his experiments in man's ability to work at depths of 1,500 ft., he also used the 600.

The 600 is carved from one block of steel, equipped with an immensely strong tempered glass, and has a special twin-locking crown. It is waterproof to 2,000 ft.

Besides the 600, Omega build a wide range of waterproof watches, all of which go through severe tests before they leave the factory. In pressure tanks, the watches are subjected to the equivalent of a leap from the bottom of the sea to twice the height of Mt. Everest; and this leap is repeated for hours on end.

Is it any wonder that experienced professionals and demanding amateurs have faith in the waterproof qualities of their Omega watches?

Ω OMEGA

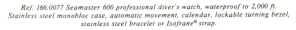

Ref. 166.0077 Seamaster 600 professional diver's watch, waterproof to 2,000 ft.
Stainless steel monobloc case, automatic movement, calendar, lockable turning bezel, stainless steel bracelet or Isofrane® strap.

Advertising for Omega's Ploprof, introduced in 1970, emphasises the model's reliability as a professional tool.

— THE 1970s

Movado Museum watch, with its indexless dial, is housed in the permanent collections of numerous museums around the world, including the Museum of Modern Art, New York.

The watch was admired, and, starting in 1977, the first limited edition was followed by one produced for sale.

Thus the "Bvlgari Bvlgari", also known as "BB", was born. The model was distinguished by a five-millimetre-thick ($1/5$-inch-thick) cylindrical case enclosing a minimalist black dial surrounded by a polished metal bezel; the shape was simple yet also well defined, with the added decorative element of an inscription to make it even more recognisable.

NEW HORIZONS

Despite the crisis that hit watchmaking between the end of the seventies and the beginning of the eighties, Vacheron Constantin positioned itself in the high-end sector, producing a limited number of pieces, all animated by mechanical movements or enhanced by complications, while also turning its attention to jewellery watches. Research in the realm originated with the Kallista, created by the maker in 1979: this watch was produced from a one-kilogramme (approx. two-pound) gold ingot and adorned with 118 diamonds for a total of 130 carats. It required six thousand hours of work and five years to construct and was one of the most expensive watches of all time.

Many fashion houses put their best industrial skills into play, giving life to fundamental innovations in technological research. This also provided a new impetus for the revolution started by high-frequency movements, which had already been the subject of horologists' work by the end of the 1960s.

Longines did not abandon its production of mechanical movements, and in 1977 it introduced the automatic Calibre L990, whose double barrel was only 2.95 millimetres ($1/8$ inch) thick (the thinnest in the world at the time of its launch), with hours, minutes, seconds and the date. In these years, the *maison* also took up its original aesthetic ambitions and brought a series of important models to the market: the Flore Marine in 1970, the Cleopatra in 1975, and the Volubilis in 1978. In 1972, they also began a collaboration with the French designer Serge Manzon, who designed a series of silver watches, characterised by geometric cases with large rounded, glossy or satin-finished surfaces made in limited series.

TAG Heuer Monaco wrist chronograph, automatic chronograph in steel, with registers and date, c. 1970.

Amid such heterogeneous offerings, Movado created the new edition of a model dating back to 1947, the Museum watch. Designed by Nathan George Horwitt, an artist trained at the Bauhaus school, its stylised dial featured a single dot at 12 o'clock, symbolising the sun at noon, and it is still recognised as an icon of modernity today.

In 1970, the maker TAG Heuer launched its Monaco model. With its distinctive square case, the Monaco was the first automatic chronograph wristwatch produced in that shape. The name of the model was inspired by the famous Formula 1 race held every spring in the principality of the same name. The Swiss company had already introduced the Carrera chronograph in the mid-1960s, and chronographs by the *maison* were all baptised with the names of famous motor racing circuits. Actor Steve McQueen wore a TAG Heuer Monaco chronograph while filming the 1971 film *Le Mans*.

THE RETURN OF MECHANICAL WATCHES

With the crisis of the 1970s, the export value of Swiss timepieces contracted, and the market share of Swiss-made watches decreased. However, while Japanese companies focused mainly on technological innovation, Swiss makers paid more attention to the further development of mechanics and marketing strategies.

The traditional watchmaking industry was reborn in part thanks to a streamlining of production systems; it was also due to the positioning of mechanical watches within the high-end market, as opposed to models produced in Asia, which had instead conquered the wider, but entry-level, market range.

In this context, the revolutionary ideas of entrepreneur Nicolas George Hayek would make their way and relaunch the Swiss market, altering the future of modern watchmaking.

The mechanical watch market would not only experience a recovery. Specialists in the sector would at the same time recognise an ever-increasing interest in rediscovering historical pieces, with numerous customers willing to purchase vintage mechanical watches. The first wristwatch auctions would make way for the phenomenon of collecting.

1970

Ploprof
Omega 1970

Since their launch in 1948, Omega Seamaster timepieces have established themselves globally thanks to their characteristics of reliability and resistance, represented in their signature hippocampus logo.

According to official Omega documentation, it took more than four years to develop a suitable solution for creating a watch that could withstand the extreme pressure of diving to great depths.

In 1970, Omega launched a watch created to withstand the terrible pressure to which divers operating in the depths of the ocean are subjected: this was the Seamaster 600, the so-called "Ploprof" (from the first letters of the words *plongeurs professionnels*, meaning "professional divers"). It is one of the strongest and most resistant underwater models ever made, ideal for use in the abyss. The model was made of steel, with a one-piece case equipped with a tempered mineral crystal and twin-locking crown.

In 2009, Omega introduced a fitted version of the Calibre 8500 with coaxial escapement. The new Ploprof 1200M is, as the name suggests, water-resistant to a depth of 1,200 metres (3,937 feet). In the Ploprof case, the screw-in crown is situated at 9 o'clock and protected by a special buffer. Its unusual location allows the wearer to move their wrist more freely and thus prevents any involuntary manipulation of the crown.

Watch with 55-by-44mm (2⅕-by-1⁷⁄₁₀in) steel monobloc case with locking mechanism to fix the bezel adjustment and winding crown, blue dial with date window at 3 o'clock, Arabic numerals and luminescent hands, black bi-directional bezel.

— THE 1970s

Explorer II
Rolex 1971

In 1971, Rolex introduced the Explorer II, which was able to provide even greater reliability in terms of chronometric precision, legibility and robustness.

The arrow-shaped hand of the Explorer II makes one revolution of the dial per day and is read using the fixed, graduated bezel. It can indicate a second time zone or provide the time according to the 24-hour clock. The model boasts a high legibility both day and night, thanks to the luminescence of the dial and the large size of its hands, including the orange 24-hour hand. This allows the wearer to distinguish the time during the day or at night, even in geographical areas or specific locations where it is difficult to distinguish between day and night, such as the polar regions or in caves.

Today the Explorer II is made with Oystersteel, a highly resistant alloy with a unique lustre. The Oyster case guarantees water resistance, and the Oyster bracelet is supplied with the Easylink extension, allowing it to be lengthened by five millimetres ($^1/_5$ inch).

The Explorer II is another example of a professional watch that has been sought by the wider public.

Watch with 40mm (1⅜in) case and extendable steel bracelet, black dial, luminescent white indices and hands, and orange, arrow-shaped 24-hour hand.

Royal Oak
Audemars Piguet 1972

Legend has it that, when looking to draw inspiration, Gérald Genta recalled when, as a child, he had seen divers wearing helmets and diving suits. The helmet had been fixed by eight bolts, and there were exactly eight hexagonal screws appearing on the model he created for Audemars Piguet in 1972.

The octagonal shape of the bezel, on the other hand, is taken from the design of the cannon mouths of the HMS *Royal Oak*, a warship launched in 1862 and the flagship of the British Royal Navy.

The particularities of the Royal Oak watch's design, the steel of which it was made, and its 39-millimetre (1½-inch) diameter, much larger than the standard dimensions of the past, made it an innovative product, and therefore difficult for the public to understand. The model was presented at Basel in 1972 and produced in a thousand examples. With its steel case, octagonal bezel, and integrated bracelet, the Royal Oak subverted the aesthetic codes of the time. To these features, refined hand-polished and satin finishes are added to reinforce its aesthetic lines and guilloché dial with a Tapisserie pattern. In 1976, the Royal Oak for women was made, and, in 1982, the quartz model. Starting in the mid-eighties, the Royal Oak would be offered with complications of various kinds, in limited series, and in jewellery editions. As a sponsor of prestigious sailing regattas, the *maison* also created celebratory versions for competitions and their winners.

To celebrate the Royal Oak's fortieth anniversary in 2012, Audemars Piguet introduced a model that was innovative while coming as close as possible to the original design by Gérald Genta. From this concept came the Royal Oak Extra-Thin tourbillon. The extra-thin self-winding mechanical movement Calibre 2121, with a date aperture, is no more than 3.05 millimetres ($^1/_{10}$ inch) thick.

Watch with 39mm (1½in) case and integrated bracelet in brushed steel, blue Tapisserie dial, applied indices, baton hands, and a date aperture at 3 o'clock.

1972

— THE 1970s

Nautilus
Patek Philippe   1976

In 1976, Patek Philippe presented the Nautilus model. Sports watches of this model "work as well with a wet suit as they do with a dinner suit", according to an advertising campaign of the time. The watch, innovative in comparison to the watchmaker's classic offerings, was conceived in collaboration with the designer Gérald Genta. Inspired by the luxurious ocean liners of the time, he designed a case modelled precisely on the shape of the ocean liners' portholes. The watch is distinguished by its cushion-shaped bezel, its dial embossed with horizontal stripes, and the integrated bracelet, made up of H-shaped and curved, pearl-like links alternating between matt and glossy finishes. Its name refers to the watch's underwater resistance, an unusual feature for a Patek Philippe model.

In production from 1981 to 2006, the reference 3800 is the smaller version of the original Nautilus reference 3700. For its thirtieth anniversary in 2006, the design of the Nautilus men's collection was subtly reworked and commemorated with the launch of the reference 5980/1A with a flyback chronograph complication, with automatic winding, and the reference 5712, also available in white or rose gold, with a leather strap. The hinges of the case have an updated design that softens its curves; the proportions and finishes of its bracelet offer improved wearability, while the indices and baton hands are slightly larger.

In 2010, the reference 5726 was enhanced with an annual calendar complication. The most impressive among the Nautilus models is the reference 5980, with a steel case 44 millimetres/$1^{7}/_{10}$ inch), water-resistant to 120 metres (393 feet), and the chronograph movement Calibre CH 28-520 C, equipped with a new instant-change date.

Watch with 42mm ($1^{7}/_{10}$in) case and steel bracelet, horizontal engraved dial. The hour and minute hands are white-gold batons with a luminescent coating, like its indices, which are easily read even in poor lighting.

Bvlgari Bvlgari
Bulgari 1977

It was 1975 when the Roman fashion house first introduced a watch with its logo: it was a limited edition, with a yellow-gold case and the inscriptions "Bvlgari" and "Roma" engraved on the bezel. It was not to be put on the market, but gifted to the brand's 100 top customers at Christmas.

From there, thanks to simple word of mouth, high demand for the unique timepiece grew, and in 1977 the first Bvlgari Bvlgari collection was born. The design is tied to the city of Rome and to Italian art and architecture: the geometry of the cylindrical case recalls the columns of ancient Roman monuments, while the bezel is inspired by coins on which the emperor's name was engraved on the outer edge, leaving the centre free for his likeness. Over the years, the Bvlgari Bvlgari has been offered in a wide variety of editions and sizes: in 18-carat yellow and white gold; in steel with a leather strap in a wide range of colours; or with a gold or steel bracelet. The watch is also available with chronograph functions and in a version with *petites complications*.

In 2004, two limited-edition Bvlgari Bvlgari watches were produced: the Tourbillon and the Minute Repeater.

In 2006 the new generation of Bvlgari Bvlgari watches was launched: the one presented at Baselworld had a completely revised design, made possible by the extensive expertise in watch production that the company had acquired. Its curved case and sophisticated dial were in fact completely developed and produced by the Bulgari Group. In addition, the extra-thin movement had a power reserve of seventy-two hours when manually wound.

In 2007, also in Basel, various models were presented with a white-gold or rose-gold case embellished with brilliant-cut diamonds, with an anthracite dial, decorated with a guilloché soleil treatment.

Watch with 33mm (1³/₁₀in) gold case, engraved bezel, black dial and leather strap.

THE 1970s —

1977

The 1980s

Between Gold and Colour

The 1980s was a decade of wellbeing and prosperity, even opulence, and one of exaggeration and narcissism. The climate of social struggle characterising the previous years contrasted with this era of highly ambitious yuppies, career women and hedonistic lifestyles.

These were also the "pop" years: design of the period stood out for its decisive, provocative character. In Milan, the Memphis Group came together. This Italian post-modernist design and architecture collective subverted the concept of "good taste", upholding bright, lively colours and geometric shapes while creating objects from low-cost materials such as plastic laminate. These were elevated through design, where conceptual complexity and a search for the cutting edge hid behind an image of simplicity and cheer.

Design and fashion became a codified form of social communication: furniture, clothes and accessories were no longer purchased according to individual desires, but based on the lifestyle that one wished to manifest.

The formal but exaggerated style chosen by "yuppies" (*y*oung *u*rban *p*rofessionals) – young people with careers, interested in earning fabulous sums within a short period of time – included pinstripes and double-breasted garments with voluminous shoulders. Shirts had high but short-pointed collars, often striped or two-tone, and worn with wide ties and braces; accessories included tie clips, cufflinks and, of course, wristwatches. Wristwatches especially became an accessory through which businessmen would communicate their success. One unforgettable figure was the character of Gordon Gekko from the film *Wall Street* (1987), who sports a Cartier Santos with a gold bracelet. In more informal contexts, light-toned suits were worn over

◀ *Michael Douglas played the ambitious trader Gordon Gekko in the film* Wall Street, *directed by Oliver Stone in 1987.*

— THE 1980s

T-shirts. "Preppy" fashion spread in the casual style of these years, featuring polo shirts with upturned collar and sweaters (often brightly coloured) worn on one's shoulders.

This context consolidated the success of all the major Italian fashion designers: Giorgio Armani, Ottavio Missoni, Gianfranco Ferré, Gianni Versace, Valentino, Salvatore Ferragamo, Moschino, Enrico Coveri, Miuccia Prada and Krizia. Thanks to their brands, "made in Italy" spread worldwide.

The first watches offered by fashion brands were also born in the 1980s. International fashion houses had already begun to diversify their offerings, and, alongside clothing, shoes, linens, jewellery and furnishings, they would also introduce watch series. Chanel and Hermès were among the first fashion *maisons* to offer wristwatches, soon followed by many others. It was in the 1980s that "fashion" watches began to contribute to the representation of a brand's style.

THE BIRTH OF THE SWATCH PHENOMENON

As fashion and design increasingly came to express personality as well as social status, an entirely new kind of watch burst onto the scene. Traditionally, a Swiss-made mechanical watch was considered an object of value to be handed down from generation to generation, synonymous with painstaking craftsmanship. In this context, the entrepreneur Nicolas G. Hayek had the idea of offering a "second watch", or "Swatch": not an expensive object of high-end horology, but an item that was new and ex-

citing. Since it didn't cost a fortune, a second watch was to be followed by a third, a fourth, and so on. If gold, enamels and precious stones were the favoured materials of traditional watchmaking, here plastic, with its multifaceted capacities, was used for an experiment unequalled in the sector.

Thanks to its flexibility and eclectic nature, plastic could be suitably combined with other materials like beads, feathers, rhinestones, glass, and metals. It could also take on infinite colour variations, allowing designers to continually update models in a perpetual metamorphosis.

The Swatch story is one of a revolution that forever changed the concept of what a watch is, and how it is worn.

Swatches were a graceful provocation of the Watch with a capital "W". Yet they also became a tool of creative expression; precious materials were replaced by plastic, a light, pristine design took the place of a hefty one, and its intrinsic value was replaced by that of an object prized for its relative uniqueness. What made Swatches precious was their constant state of transformation. The series of metamorphoses gave birth to watches that could each interpret – and even predict – the many forms of contemporary thought and taste. The first Swatch was released in March 1983, and the market response proved to be exceptional. After its first models with a classic round case, now called "Swatch Originals", an impressive series of collections followed. By January 1984, the number of pieces sold had already reached one million; in 1985, the ten-millionth watch was produced.

Apart from its classic function of marking the time, the Swatch became an accessory in every sense, an accessory that could be chosen, bought and replaced according to one's style of dress, curiosity or of-the-moment inspiration.

Hayek's "second watch" was never just a watch. It has also always been a tool of communication, a conversation piece designed to allow wearers to express their identities and emotions.

In 1986, the POP Swatch was launched: very different from the standard models, its case had nearly double the diameter of the others, and its strap was much wider and softer. Its distinguishing feature was that it came with interchangeable supports. In 1989 the Oigol Oro model was released as part of the Swatch Art Specials series; it was designed by Mimmo Paladino, an artist of the Italian *transavanguardia*, produced in only 120 examples and distributed to personalities from the world of politics, culture, entertainment and sport – this included Mikhail Gorbachev, Stephen King, Renzo Piano and Madonna.

Hedonism on Display

The 1980s have been called the "golden years", and, certainly, gold was employed profusely.

The Oigol Oro model from the Swatch Art Specials series, designed by Mimmo Paladino. *This model would reach record figures at auction. The Oigol Oro (reading orologio, Italian for "watch", in reverse) shows a touch of theatre: on the white surface of the dial is the image of a devilish creature with horns, his red trident indicating the time. Drawn with thoughtful, ironic restraint, this lively and charming Mephistopheles has the grace and dark charm of an on-stage character.*

— THE 1980s

The king of precious metals featured not only in luxury watches, but in sports models as well. Jewellery watches with sporty designs could be glimpsed on the wrists of Arab and Texan oil magnates, kings and entrepreneurs, Hollywood actors and directors. This category included a luxury version of the Rolex reference 6269, produced in limited numbers. Made of gold, with a dial and bezel set with diamonds, the watch was made to capture attention. Another trend that characterised sports models' aesthetic was a combination of gold and steel in both the watch case and bracelet: these two-tone models recalled the timepieces of the thirties and forties, but with a look much more oriented towards a striking contrast than to a sense of harmony. Select models by Rolex, Omega and Audemars Piguet were offered in this combination.

A New Elegance

Although the market was dominated by mass-produced quartz watches, and increasingly by experimental designer models, at the end of the 1970s and beginning of the 1980s there was also a strong demand for classic models: watches that needed to be reliable and durable, with a modern aesthetic.

Some watchmakers took up the styles of past eras via contemporary reinterpretations: in 1985, Cartier presented the Pasha, inspired by its ancestor from the 1930s, which had been specially constructed by Cartier at the request of Thami El Glaoui, Pasha of Marrakesh. In 1983, the *maison* also introduced the Panthère watch. The model's name comes from its bracelet, whose ultra-flexible construction recalls the movements of the maker's feline emblem.

Panthère de Cartier wristwatch, small model. Cartier, 1983. Gold with cabochon sapphire. Quartz movement, round, Côtes de Genève motif, 4 rubies.
This is one of the first examples of the Panthère de Cartier, a model launched in 1983. Cartier collection.

In 1982, Longines celebrated its 150th anniversary with an ultra-thin collection featuring a gold case, dubbed Agassiz in honour of Auguste Agassiz, founder of the *maison*. This model was the progenitor of the La Grande Classique collection that would be introduced in the 1990s.

In 1989, Vacheron Constantin presented five collections: Phidias, with a sporty, technical design; Les Historiques, which drew inspiration from the company's tradition; Les Absolues, which included high-end jewellery pieces; Les Essentielles, referencing a classic style; and, finally, the Les Complications line, which marked the company's return to deepening its technical expertise by focusing on complications.

Attention to past styles was also to be found at Omega. While the Constellation had been conceived as a precision chronograph in 1952, thirty years later, in 1982, the Constellation Manhattan first featured the famous "claws" that would come to symbolise the collection.

To celebrate its 150th anniversary in 1989, Patek Philippe introduced its Officier model, inspired by wristwatches from the first decade of the twentieth century.

Classic watches of the 1950s provided a source of inspiration for the new Portofino collection, introduced by IWC in 1984, with a yellow-gold case and silver dial, but with the completely modern feature of a 46-millimetre (1⅘-inch) case diameter. In 1985, Schaffhausen presented the Da Vinci, a mechanical chronograph with a perpetual calendar, a fully mechanical set-up and a four-digit display up to the year 2499. Despite its complex mechanism, the watch was simple to use, as adjustments to the date, day of the week, month, year, decade, century, millennium and moon-phase indications were all synchronised, day by day, and could be made by means of the winding crown. In 1988, for the manufacture's 120th anniversary, IWC introduced the reference 2532, a timepiece with a gold case, IWC Calibre 4231 manual-winding movement, a dial with Roman numerals, small seconds, and a sapphire crystal.

With the emergence of quartz at the end of the 1970s, the Swiss watch industry was in complete crisis. Aware of the fact that a mechanical watch could not compete with a quartz watch in terms of price, many makers decided to relaunch the field

18-carat yellow-gold wristwatch with original yellow-gold buckle. Produced as a limited edition of 2,000 examples to celebrate the 150th anniversary of Patek Philippe in 1989.

of mechanical watchmaking by reinstating complications as a differentiating feature in products of the highest quality.

In 1984, Audemars Piguet created the Royal Oak with a perpetual calendar, while in 1986 the company introduced the first ultra-thin wristwatch housing an automatic tourbillon movement.

In the 1980s, Blancpain introduced timepieces

that were aesthetically highly elegant and technically daring; these included the Villeret Minute Repeater and the Villeret Chronograph, both from 1987.

The Trilogy of Time

In the early 1980s, the Swiss businessman Rolf W. Schnyder, who had always been fond of mechanical watches, purchased the Ulysse Nardin factory in order to restore it to its former glory.

The project to reintroduce the *maison* began with the idea of creating a watch that had never been made before. This led to the introduction in 1985 of the Astrolabium Galileo Galilei model. Just like an astrolabe, it indicated the positions of the Sun, Moon, and stars at all times from a specific point on the Earth; it showed the rising and setting of both the Sun and the Moon, solar and lunar eclipses, the month, and the date. The Astrolabium was followed, a few years later, by the Planetarium Copernicus, an astronomical wristwatch indicating the time through the movements of the planets in the solar system. This complex watch brought together both the geocentric conception of Ptolemy, positioning the Earth at the centre of the universe, and the heliocentric conception of Copernicus, who instead placed the Sun at the centre, uniting them within a single instrument. This combination of the two philosophies made it possible to establish the position of principal planets relative to the Sun and the Earth. Here, the Moon revolves around the Earth, and the perpetual calendar displaying the months and signs of the zodiac completes a rotation in 365.24 days. These two watches, together with the Tellurium Johannes Kepler, a 1992 watch that would tell the time using a specific reading of the Earth's rotation, constitute what is still called the "trilogy of time".

With the market for mechanical watches resuming, models with grand complications came onto the scene. These combined a series of various functions within a single watch: chronographs, perpetual calendars, or world time complications allowing one to tell the time in 24 time zones.

In 1985, Patek Philippe returned to grand complications with the reference 3940, the first ultra-thin perpetual calendar watch put into regular production. The watch later became one of the maker's classic models. The following year, the company patented the secular perpetual calendar with a retrograde date.

In 1989, to celebrate its 150th anniversary, Patek Philippe presented the most complicated watch in the world: the Calibre 89. This pocket watch, made up of 1,728 components, sported thirty-three complications, including a secular calendar accounting for the Gregorian calendar's omission of three leap days every four hundred years.

The Birth of Collecting

Until the 1980s, the collectors' market for vintage wristwatches was virtually non-existent. There was a limited bibliography, and few resources existed for research; therefore, collectors had little knowledge of how vintage pieces were produced. Interest in the rediscovery of historical pieces was growing markedly, however. The Genevan auction house Galerie genevoise d'horlogerie ancienne, founded by Osvaldo Patrizzi and Gabriel Tortella in 1974, was a pioneer in the field of auctions dedicated to watches. In April 1981, it organised the first auction entirely dedicated to wristwatches. This was followed by themed auctions dedicated to individual brands, for instance "The Art of Patek Philippe", held in 1989, the year of the prestigious watchmaker's 150th anniversary, and "The Art of Breguet" in 1991. In addition to detailed information on the featured watches, its innovative catalogue included the historical background and biographies of their famous owners, thus tracing a history of the maker through its most prestigious and illustrious customers over the course of two centuries. Other auctions were organised to provide an overview of the watchmaking production of a particular country. "L'art de l'horlogerie en France", held in 1993, chronicled the historical evolution of French watchmaking from 1500 to modern times, while "The Art of British Horology", held two years afterwards, illustrated the development path of English watchmaking.[1] Within a short time, large auction houses restructured to open specialised divisions and organise auctions dedicated to timepieces.

The market in the 1980s was chaotic, notes Daryn Schnipper, chairman of the International Watch Division of Sotheby's, and enthusiasts were animatedly debating what values made a watch collectible: the brand, or the style; its mechanical complexity, or its historical relevance? The answer to this question has evolved multiple times over the years. In the end, collectors were in agreement in terms of using the brand as a point of reference.[2] The detailed study of vintage wristwatches by early enthusiasts gradually led to knowledge being spread among an increasingly wider audience, and buyers, becoming increasingly better versed, began to consciously purchase the pieces they wished to add to their collections.

The rapid development of the vintage wristwatch market did not escape the attention of the makers, which in the following decades began to introduce new models inspired by their past iconic and historical models.

---

[1] PATRIZZI, OSVALDO - CAPPELLETTI, MARA, *Investing in Wristwatches: Rolex*, ACC Art Books, Woodbridge 2021.

[2] SCHNIPPER, DARYN, *The Wristwatch Comes of Age*, in PATRIZZI, OSVALDO - CAPPELLETTI, MARA, *op. cit.*

— THE 1980s

1986

POP
Swatch 1986

The "POP" Swatch came onto the market in the winter of 1986–1987, launched as a playfully provocative challenge.

It was very different from other Swatches: the case's diameter was nearly doubled, and the strap was much wider and softer, therefore able to adapt to any wrist. A POP watch could also be removed from the strap and worn directly on one's clothing, thanks to a clip fixed to its case. It was also supplied with three other accessories: a chain that transformed it into a pocket watch, a magnet that could attach it to any metal surface, and an adhesive strip that could attach it to non-metal surfaces.

Its name was a clear reference to pop art – colourful, fun and within everyone's reach – with its natural links to the concept of reproducibility. Swatch watches, like Andy Warhol's portraits, theoretically can be reproduced indefinitely, but in practice are produced in limited quantities. What has made them precious is their continuous transformation; the series of metamorphoses from which these objects have emerged has been able to interpret and even anticipate the myriad forms of thought and taste of the time.

The name POP was also onomatopoeic, as the case could "pop" in and out of its supports.

Today POP watches are housed in museums and belong to private collections all over the world. They have been passed from one collector to the next as precious relics – souvenirs of the crazy, hyperbolic and exciting decade when Swatches were born: the 1980s.

Watch with 44mm (1⁷/₁₀in) transparent plastic case displaying its quartz movement, waterproof down to 30m (98ft), black pencil hands, soft silicone strap with buckle fastening.

— THE 1980s

Pasha
Cartier 1985

In 1933, Louis Cartier received a request from Thami El Glaoui, Pasha of Marrakesh and a well-known figure among the international jet set. El Glaoui, one of the most famous pashas in Morocco, wanted a watch that was water-resistant so he could also wear it in his swimming pool.

Louis Cartier, who already counted many high-profile leaders among his clients, accepted the pasha's request and built a timepiece to his specifications, first among them the waterproof rectangular case.

The watch remained one of the few waterproof watches until 1943, when Cartier began to produce a large gold model with a round, water-resistant case that featured a grid over the dial for shock protection, its inspiration coming from the military watches used in the First World War. The Pasha was named in honour of their first waterproof model, but also as a tribute to luxury and refinement. The Pasha watch of today, however, was introduced in 1985, when Cartier, revisiting the 1943 design, created a model of larger proportions, and, to ensure that the crown was waterproof, decided to cover it with a small cap, embellished with a classic Cartier cabochon and attached to the case by a link.

In 1991, the first steel Pasha was introduced, and, in 1995, Cartier created the Pasha C line at a lower price, without a sapphire cabochon.

Pasha de Cartier wristwatch with self-winding movement and rotating bezel, 38mm (1½in) Cartier, 1986.

Gold, one sapphire cabochon, leather strap. Notched winding crown made waterproof by a screw cap. Round self-winding movement, date, Côtes de Genève decoration, rhodium-plated, 17 jewels, shock-resistant, Swiss lever escapement, monometallic balance, flat balance spring.

The rotating bezel enables a diver to assess the time spent under water. The triangle is aligned with the minute hand, which then indicates elapsed diving time by the numerals engraved on the bezel.

This is one of the earliest examples of the Pasha de Cartier, a model launched in 1985. Cartier Collection.

THE 1980s —

1985

— THE 1980s

1987

Villeret Répétition Minutes (reference 6036-3442-55B)
Blancpain 1987

The minute repeater is one of the major complications in the art of watchmaking. Originally conceived to indicate the time in the dark, it is still one of the most fascinating and complex complications today. Pressing the button controlling this complication, triggers a chime, which strikes the hours, quarter hours and minutes. The repetition mechanism must accurately "read" the time indicated by the watch and transform it into a precise number of strokes. This can be complex, especially due to the slight difference between the hours indicated, for example between 12:59:59 and 1:00:00. For this reason, the mechanism's components must be assembled with an extremely reduced tolerance and with extreme precision. This is incredible, if we consider that the assembly and adjustments are done manually.

Other challenges to a refined repeating-strike mechanism are purity of sound and musicality. There is no fixed design to achieve this, and there are no computer formulae or secret recipes. Perfection is achieved through fine adjustments of the hand and a selection of the best metals to form the hammers and "bells".

In the development of the Calibre 35 in 1987, Blancpain further pushed the boundaries of what was already considered one of the most complex complications to make, creating the smallest and thinnest minute repeater in the world, also equipped with an automatic wind. Some of its hand-finished components are finer than a human hair.

The Villeret Répétition Minutes watch (reference 6036-3442-55B) is equipped with the automatic Calibre 35 with a minute repeater. It has a 38mm (1½in) platinum case, an opalescent dial, Roman indices, and a crocodile strap.

Villeret Chronographe (reference 4082-1542-55)
Blancpain 1987

Chronographs have always occupied an important place in the collections by Blancpain. Several models are available with two push-pieces, or in a monopusher version. Beginning with the chronograph function, Blancpain has historically developed complementary complications like the split-second or flyback, or alternatively combined the chronograph with other complications, creating for instance perpetual-calendar and tourbillon chronographs.

In 1987, the Brassus *maison* developed the Calibre 1185; it was, at the time, the flattest automatic chronograph movement in the world. The start, stop and reset functions of the chronograph took place by means of a column wheel device, a solid cylindrical component with six trapezoidal "columns" formed at the top; these serve to manage the levers controlling the chronograph's functions.

This system ensures that the chronograph starts smoothly. For this movement, Blancpain developed a vertical clutch that operated its two overlapping seconds wheels: when the start button was pressed, the clutch engaged the mechanism via smooth contact with these two discs. This solution eliminated sudden jumps of the hand when the chronograph was running, without negatively affecting the accuracy of the running watch.

Thanks to the Calibre 1185, the Villeret Chronographe, reference 4082-1542-55, was the thinnest automatic chronograph in the world. It is distinguished by the stepped bezel of its case, by its chronograph push-pieces of moderate size, and by a dial with prominent applied Roman numerals.

Villeret Chronographe with 40mm (1⅜in) white gold case, opalescent dial with applied Roman indices, and two counters. Automatic movement Calibre 1185 with chronograph function; crocodile strap.

THE 1980s —

1987

The 1990s

Minimalist Luxury

The 1990s distanced themselves from the previous decade's ostentation. New consumers were seeking objects' intrinsic value, derived from workmanship and history, yet without flaunting them.

An elegance of refined simplicity came to the fore during these years, inspired by the concept of "less is more" found in architecture, figurative art, and literature.

Minimalist architects and designers, including Peter Zumthor, John Pawson, Naoto Fukasawa, Tadao Ando and Jasper Morrison, responded, in their own way, to the previous decade's industry excesses by embracing new design philosophies. As Pawson would explain, "Minimalism is not an architecture of self-denial, deprivation, or absence: it is defined not by what is not there, but by the rightness of what is there and by the richness with which this is experienced."

In the late 1990s and early 2000s, Morrison and Fukasawa developed the concept of the "Super Normal", a term they used to praise everyday design objects that fulfilled their functions in an extraordinary way, making them a pleasure to use.

Urban Style

From Seattle, a city completely outside the fashion circuit, came the style of grunge, its look made up of brushed-cotton shirts, ripped jeans, caps, T-shirts, knitted cardigans, and Converse shoes. This style also influenced fashion on the catwalks in various interpretations, unveiling a so-called "urban" style, combining

◀ *Pierce Brosnan, symbol of the glamorous elegance of the 1990s, played James Bond from 1995 to 2002. Onscreen, he wore an Omega Seamaster Diver 300M.*

sportswear with classic garments. In menswear, paying homage to more minimalist dress, single-breasted jacket styles were deconstructed to the point of transformation into pullover jackets that adhered to the body; these were worn with straight, non-pleated trousers. A soft, lightweight version of the button-up shirt lost its collar, while crewneck T-shirts and turtlenecks were worn under jackets. Fabric colours were neutral and natural: white, beige, grey and black, and often in subtle tones.

Casualwear, with its roots in multiculturalism, became a starting point for infinite modifications which made it fashionable. This style was fit for "metrosexuals", a term born in the nineties to define a generation of heterosexual men living in big cities who were very attentive to their appearance. At the same time, the concept of "vintage" was also spreading, with garments of the past being admired once again for their style.

The taste for this new, less showy elegance was also present in watches, and it had a great impact on the aesthetics of the decade's new pieces.

Cartier, which revisited the Tank in the late 1980s and early 1990s, was exemplary in this respect. The company introduced the Tank Américaine in 1988; its style was closer to that of its American customers, who preferred larger watches. In 1996, the *maison* introduced the first Tank Française collection, which included twelve models, offered in three band types: 18-carat polished yellow gold, 18-carat yellow gold and steel, and alligator skin.

Tank Américaine wristwatch, Cartier, 1993. Gold, faceted sapphire, and leather strap. Round movement, Côtes de Genève decoration, rhodium-plated, 5 adjustments, 18 jewels, shockproof, Swiss anchor escapement, monometallic balance wheel, flat balance spring. Cartier Collection.

In 1997, a model with a steel bracelet was introduced. The chain bracelet was a hallmark of its design, developed for a younger audience that paid attention to detail.

"Parallel to experimenting with materials, a study of form was taking place, looking to a 'conceptual' luxury continuously stimulated by a combination of design, graphics, art, and fashion."[1]

---

[1] CAPPELLETTI, MARA, *Un quadrilatero d'oro*, in "Stilemilano – Storie di eleganza", Exhibition Catalogue, Nexo, Milan 2020, p. 43.

Between Art and Fashion

In this context, witnessing an ever-stronger link between the luxury object and applied arts, Swatch enjoyed enormous success. At this time, the company strengthened its connection to the art world by developing the concept of Swatch collecting. Its watches were always offered at an accessible price but in limited, highly valued series. Painters, sculptors, musicians and directors tried their hand with these objects of design. There were many creative collaborations; among the most significant were those with Keith Haring, Alfred Hofkunst, Jean-Michel Folon, Mimmo Paladino, Mimmo Rotella, Akira Kurosawa, Spike Lee, Renzo Piano and Moby. An integral part of each Swatch Art Special Edition was its packaging, which was often as fun and original as the watches themselves. The year 1990 was a very significant one in the history of Swatch, as it saw the launch of the Scuba and Chrono. The new models were immediately in high demand, with long queues and waiting lists created to snatch the new items in Swatch flagship stores. In 1991, its first three Automatics were introduced; this was an important evolution of the Swatch, since it was mechanical, no longer quartz. Moving from innovation to innovation, the Swatch, born of plastic, turned to metal in 1995 with the introduction of the Irony collection. What else could the *maison* in Biel invent? A flatter Swatch. *Voilà*: in 1997, the Skin appeared, 3.9 millimetres (1/8 inch) thick. Then, a larger model: in 2002 came the X-Large, thirty per cent larger than the usual Swatch size. Swatch's trademark material, plastic, took centre stage once again in the Chrono Plastic, offered in a wide range of colours, new shapes, and new dimensions.[2]

Swatch's experimentation has continued over the years, in terms of material, technique and shape, following what one could call an enduring creative revolution.

The Italian artist and poet Mimmo Rotella, perhaps best known for his collages, worked by tearing and destroying the surface of vintage posters and advertisements so that segments of time could emerge from their multiple layers. For Swatch, the urban archaeologist selected a "real" Marilyn, freed from the patinaed gravure of her legacy.

With its vintage advertising palette and juxtapositions (or contradictions), the work focuses on the star's personality, exploring points where the image has been torn. Marilyn *by Mimmo Rotella dates to 1994.*

---

[2] Cappelletti, Mara, *Swatch*, 24 Ore Cultura, Milan 2012, p. 20.

— THE 1990s

Swatch Automatic watches were presented on the market as a watch "in need of movement", but these models continue to function even in the absence of movement, boasting a power reserve of 46 hours.
 Rubin automatic watch with plastic case, featuring a transparent portion of the dial at 12 o'clock displaying the movement, with Roman numerals and baton hands. The movement's anchor is visible through an aperture at 11 o'clock, as are some of the escape wheel's teeth. Leather band.

Watches and Hollywood

The 1990s were also the decade when watchmaking companies consolidated their relationships with movie stars. In 1995, a close collaboration began between Omega and the big screen. In the movie *Golden Eye*, of the James Bond saga, Pierce Brosnan first wore a Seamaster Professional Diver 300M with a blue dial. Since then, the Seamaster has accompanied the world's most famous secret agent in all his other films: *Tomorrow Never Dies*, *The World Is Not Enough* and *Die Another Day*, as well as *Casino Royale* and *Quantum of Solace* with Bond being played by Daniel Craig. It also appeared in *Skyfall* and *Spectre*, accompanying the agent through *No Time to Die* in 2021.

Sylvester Stallone was the face of Panerai. The actor wore a Luminor, revived by the Italian manufacture, starting in 1993 on the set of the movie *Daylight*, which was shot in Italy.

In 1999, the Royal Oak Offshore "End of Days" chronograph was worn by Arnold Schwarzenegger in the film of the same name. The collaboration between Audemars Piguet and the actor would resume in 2003 in *Terminator 3: Rise of the Machines*, when he wore the Royal Oak Offshore T3 chronograph, the largest model ever made by the maker for its Offshore line. With its 57.2-millimetre-wide (2¼-inch-wide) case, the watch suited the actor's imposing physique and ensured an excellent legibility of all its functions, even at night. Chronographs by Bulgari appear on the wrists of Val Kilmer, the lead in *The Saint*, and of Johnny Depp in *Nick of Time*.

Bulgari watches would also appear in *Mission Impossible I* and *II*, *Minority Report* with Tom Cruise, and in *South Kensington* with Rupert Everett. Catherine Zeta-Jones wears a Quadrato in *Intolerable Cruelty*.

Souls *Sportif*

In 1992, Rolex introduced the Yacht-Master, a luxury sports watch dedicated to the nautical universe, particularly to that of sailors and skippers. It was a yellow-gold watch with a 40-millimetre-thick (1 3/5-inch-thick) case, a bidirectional rotating bezel, sapphire crystal, screw-down triplock crown, Oysterlock bracelet, and a Calibre 3135 movement, water resistant to 100 metres (328 feet).

Omega's Seamaster Diver 300M debuted in 1993, first as a quartz model, soon followed by automatic versions. This specific model was very elegant and sported a wave-patterned dial.

Still in the sports field, Audemars Piguet decided to create a larger edition of the Royal Oak, introducing the Royal Oak Offshore in 1993. The differences between this model and the original Royal Oak were its larger, thicker case, as the movement was inserted into a protective antimagnetic cage, and the visible gasket to ensure greater water resistance; the bezel, pushers and crown were coated with rubber.

In the field of sports watches, thick matt steel prevailed, combined with straps made of technical materials resulting from lengthy experimentation. This was the case, for example, with Patek Philippe's Aquanaut, which entered the scene in 1997.

To face the less-than-positive economic and political challenges occurring worldwide, Officine Panerai considered entering the civilian watchmaking market for the first time in 1992. It launched three distinct models, with a total of ten references in numbered, limited editions. Thus the Luminor and Luminor Marina watches, both 44 millimetres (1 7/10 inch) in diameter, and the 42-millimetre (1 7/10 inch) Mare Nostrum chronograph, were born.

Each of these models drew inspiration from the historical models developed for the Italian Navy from the 1930s.

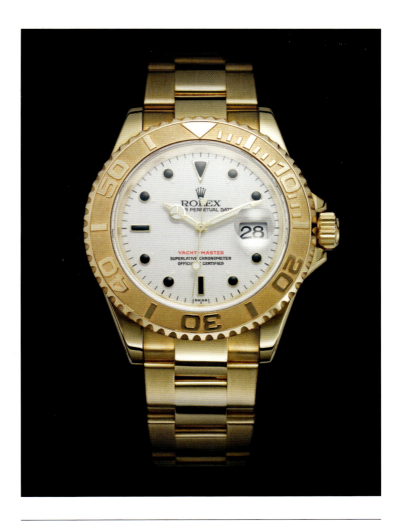

Introduced in the 1990s in yellow gold, the Yacht-Master would eventually be available in steel, platinum and Rolesor (gold and steel) editions.

This initiative could be realised thanks to top Naval officials formally relieving engineer Dino Zei, then-CEO of Officine Panerai, of the Panerai Company's commitment to military secrecy. Up to that point, such secrets had been strictly maintained and enforced for all products manufactured exclusively for military purposes, including diving watches.

On 10 September 1993, the new Panerai collection was presented at the La Spezia Naval Base, on the Italian Navy cruiser *Durand De La Penne*.

The Return of Complications

In the 1990s, many traditional brands chose to put their unparalleled excellence in craftsmanship on display by manufacturing extremely complicated mechanical timepieces. The founder was Patek Philippe, who in 1989 launched the Calibre 89 pocket watch to celebrate the 150th anniversary of the *maison*. The 1990s were significant for the maker, which in 1996 patented a watch movement with an annual calendar.

Other houses also introduced technically refined models. At Baselworld in 1990, IWC presented the "Grande Complication" wristwatch, with a perpetual calendar, chronograph and minute repeater, marking Schaffhausen's turn towards grand complications. The Destriero Scafusia was produced in 1993, on the 125th anniversary of the International Watch Co., in a limited edition of only 125 examples. It featured twenty-one functions and displays: in addition to its perpetual calendar, it featured moon phases, a minute repeater, a split-second chronograph, and a flying tourbillon.

Blancpain had entered this fascinating sector in 1991, uniting a minute repeater, tourbillon and perpetual calendar, along with the moon phase and a flyback chronograph, in its Grande Complication 1735 animated by an automatic movement. In 1998, the maker introduced the automatic Villeret Tourbillon, powered by the first self-winding tourbillon movement with an 8-day power reserve.

In the 1990s, Audemars Piguet introduced a series of both technical and stylistic innovations that would provide the company with new impetus. These included the Dual Time function, indicating the hour and minutes of two time zones in a single movement, created in 1990; and then, in 1992, the Triple Complication: a perpetual calendar chronograph with a minute repeater and 52-week indication, whose movement brought together more than twelve functions, with a total of 600 pieces. Meanwhile, the Grande Sonnerie model, from 1994, chimed on the hours and quarter-hours; it held a miniaturised movement of more than 410 pieces, with a diameter of 28.6 millimetres ($1^1/_8$ inches) and a total thickness of 5.2 millimetres ($^1/_5$ inch); it took three years of work to complete.

Also in 1995, the John Schaeffer Minute Repeater returned, as a modernised version of the first piece which had been made in 1907. That same year, the Millenary, with its characteristic elliptical shape, made its debut and would be offered in a very wide range of editions.

Important contributions to the field of grand complications also came from the Breguet workshop. At this time, Breguet introduced the Classique line, which included its *Grandes Complications* models. These allowed the master horologists at the *maison* to express their technical and creative skill, perfecting the most complex mechanisms, such as the minute repeater, tourbillon, and double tourbillon.

All these high-end timepieces proved that mechanical watchmaking was not only still in existence, but had a great future ahead of it.

In 1994 Bulgari's entry into the world of fine watchmaking was marked with the launch of two Grandes Complications: the Tourbillon and the Répétition Minutes. This marked the beginning of the fashion house's deeper journey towards fine watchmaking, dedicating itself ever further to the sector over time. The group invested heav-

Audemars Piguet's Millenary was introduced in 1995. Signature features of this watch include its elliptical case and the decentralised multi-faceted dial that reveals part of its escapement, manufactured in reverse. Women's models are often available in jewellery editions.

ily in a vertical integration strategy to make fine watchmaking the brand's reference market. Its Aluminium model, featuring a modern design and unusual materials, was launched in 1998. The case was made of aluminium and the black rubber bezel engraved with the double "Bulgari Bulgari" logo; the bracelet, also made of rubber, had aluminium joints and an aluminium buckle. For its launch, Bulgari made a deal with Alitalia to customise the body of a Boeing 747 with a faithful depiction of the Aluminium.

Other watches introduced in the 1990s have simple, refined lines and played with contrasting materials and colours. The Bulgari Rettangolo boasts a design harkening back to the simple lines of the 1930s, with a steel case and a sporty rubber strap with steel links.

The Quadrato, on the other hand, its name meaning "square", is distinguished by the shape of its case, which, enclosing a bas-relief circular motif, recalls the timeless theme of the search to "square the circle". The matt black dial is embellished with metal numerals.

New Explorations

Bringing their greatest industrial capacities into play, many makers invented fundamental technical innovations

For Eberhard & Co., the 1990s began with their introduction in 1992 of the Tazio Nuvolari chronograph, celebrating what would have been the legendary motorist's 100th birthday. For the design of this model, the maker's creatives were inspired by the finish on dashboards installed in early twentieth-century cars. The unique "rosette" workmanship underneath, fastened by screws, and on the bezel were the stylistic cues distinguishing this model, the progenitor of a series. Discerning a new trend in the market, the *maison* geared its production towards large models in 1996: one example of these is the Traversetolo, with a case 43 millimetres (1¾ inches) in diameter, followed by Grande Taille ("large") and Géant ("jumbo") editions of the Tazio Nuvolari. The company's ongoing research led, in 1997, to the creation of the 8 Jours watch, a manual mechanical model that required winding only once every eight days, thanks to a special winding device consisting of two overlapping springs.

In 1990, the master watchmakers of Jaeger-

LeCoultre created the Geographic, an automatic watch with a power reserve that simultaneously indicated the hours, minutes, seconds, local date, and, on a second dial, the time in another time zone of the wearer's choice. By selecting one of twenty-four place names and positioning it in the appropriate window via the crown, the time of the corresponding time zone was automatically set, with a distinction between day and night.

As tastes evolved following the Second World War, interest in the Reverso waned, and by 1969, when the first quartz wristwatch heralded the beginning of the biggest crisis ever faced by the Swiss watch industry, it had already been forgotten. As quartz gained ground, however, Jaeger-LeCoultre's Italian distributor Giorgio Corvo purchased the last remaining 200 Reverso cases; he inserted mechanical movements into them and sold all of them within a month. In 1975, the Reverso was officially reborn. In 1981, the company entrusted one of its engineers, Daniel Wild, with the task of redesigning the Reverso case based on modern technical standards. However, given the Reverso's classic status, any aesthetic changes had to be near-imperceptible. The new case was presented in 1985 and was the first by Jaeger-LeCoultre to be manufactured with then-new CNC technology. Resistant to water and dust, with a new flip-over mechanism, redesigned attachments for the loops and support for the case, it consisted of fifty-five components, replacing its twenty-three original ones. Stylistically, however, the watch looked exactly the same.

In 1991, sixty years after it was first produced, the Reverso began its transformation, going from "one style, one watch" to becoming a complete collection. In 1994, the Reverso Duoface was created, a singular expression of two times, with the local time on its front dial and that of one's place of residence on the other. This was followed in 1997 by the Reverso Duetto, a feminine interpretation of the double dial.

In 1991, to celebrate the bicentenary of its founding, Girard-Perregaux presented a wrist version of its celebrated "tourbillon with three gold bridges". In 1999, for its entry into the Salon International de la Haute Horlogerie, the maker introduced a self-winding version of this model.

From the early 1990s, Vacheron Constantin focused its productive and creative forces on the development of ultra-thin movements, and in 1992 it introduced the thinnest wristwatch minute-repeater calibre of its time, only 3.28 millimetres ($1/8$ inch) thick. In 1996, the company launched the Overseas collection. Its stylistic notes evoked journeys – through the fluid, decisive lines of the case, a bezel inspired by the Maltese cross, its indices and crown, its screw-down push-pieces, and its caseback, embellished with a high-relief medallion portraying the Italian Navy's famous training ship, the *Amerigo Vespucci*.

The Rebirth of German Watchmaking

Following the political and economic reunification of Germany, after nearly four decades under the GDR, prestigious German watchmaking was resurrected in the early nineties, and the town of Glashütte once again became its centre. In the early 1990s, the VEB Glashütter Uhrenbetriebe was privatised and became Glashütter Uhrenbetrieb GmbH, a limited liability company. In 1994, a private investor bought the company, aiming to combine the traditional values of German watch-

Picture showing registers by the company A. Lange & Söhne, with two versions of the Lange 1 model.
TA. Lange & Söhne officially make their watches from precious metals. Only a few pieces have been produced with stainless-steel cases, making them highly valued by collectors.

making with the most highly advanced concepts and innovations. In that same year, the maker began to sign its collections with the "Glashütte Original" trademark. It debuted in 1995 with the presentation of the Julius Assmann 1, a watch equipped with a perpetual calendar and flying tourbillon. The 1845 collection was presented the following year, with the Alfred Helwig Flying Tourbillon as its centrepiece. The year 1997 saw the debut of the Senator II line and the introduction of the Julius Assmann 2, which married a Glashütte Original mechanical movement with a dial of precious Meissen porcelain.

The re-founding of the A. Lange & Söhne workshop was also recorded at this time thanks to the efforts of Walter Lange, who designed and built the new era's first Lange watches. This is how a series of wristwatches was begun in 1994, which included the Saxonia, Tourbillon "Pour le Mérite", Arkade and Lange 1 models. These first watches already featured the stylistic and technical foundations that would characterise the maker's production in the years to come. Both in design and in technique, the *maison* established strong ties with tradition and with the territory to which it was linked. Since then, the renewed company's creative force continued to grow, until, in 1997, it presented its Langematik models, their first with an automatic movement. In 1999 they presented the Datograph, a flyback chronograph with jumping minute counters and a large date, as well as the Lange 1 Tourbillon in 2000. Since then, German makers have continued to produce a series of highly refined watches, recovering exclusive manufacturing techniques and processes.

— THE 1990s

Chrono
Swatch 1990

In the spring of 1990, Swatch launched a new line on the Swiss, Italian and French markets that caused a great stir. It was a collection of chronographs which, in addition to indicating the time, could time events with impressive precision. The chronograph made it possible to measure a single time, additional times, and intermediate times; it also had a tachymeter, allowing the user to immediately calculate an average speed per kilometre. The novelty was that these high-precision watches, thanks to quartz movements and high production volumes, were available at a low price, and therefore to a very broad audience.

Some Swatch Chrono models were offered with a date window, others without.

With fun graphics, bright colours, and the lightweight material with which they were made, the Chrono models downplayed what had always been one of the most revered objects in mechanical watchmaking: the chronograph. In the winter between 1994 and 1995, Swatch launched the Irony collection, which included watches with stainless steel or aluminium cases. In 1996, the Irony Chrono arrived boasting a chronograph function, but in a metal edition. In 2001, Swatch introduced the 6.6-millimetre-thick (¼-inch-thick) Skin Chrono.

In 2007, Swatch would introduce the Irony Chrono Retrograde. The chronograph with retrograde display was fitted with a hand that, instead of running normally along a full revolution of the dial, completed an arc along the circle, then began a new measurement after suddenly jumping back to its starting position.

Continuing the story of these models, in 2002, Diaphane Chrono watches were introduced, then Irony Chrono Automatics in 2009, and Big Bold Chrono watches in 2021.

Chrono series watch with a black, round case and grey plastic bracelet. Light grey dial with Arabic numerals; secondary dials with yellow, blue and red coloured hands; baton hour and minute hands; thin red seconds hand.

Seamaster Diver 300M
Omega 1993

The Seamaster Professional Diver 300M collection was born in 1993 and has held a prominent place in the Omega range ever since. Articulated in a variety of sizes, from 41 to 44 millimetres (1$\frac{3}{5}$ to 1$\frac{7}{8}$ inches), with black, blue and white dials, some of the Seamaster 300M's most iconic features were its helium escape valve, underwater bezel, and dial patterned with waves inspired by the sea.

The fame of this model grew from when it was worn by Pierce Brosnan as James Bond.

In 2018, on its twenty-fifth anniversary, a careful restyling updated the range in both materials and technology, while remaining faithful to its original design and the strong allure of the ocean.

The reinterpretation firstly included new dimensions, with a diameter of 42 millimetres (1$\frac{5}{8}$ inches), a ceramic bezel with a graduated scale in Ceragold (a material blending ceramic and 18-carat gold) or white enamel, the return of the famous wave pattern on its dial, and a new, conical shape for the helium escape valve.

The wave motif, which adorned the model's first dials in its early years and was subsequently abandoned, is back in the spotlight, created through laser engraving on the ceramic of the dial. Ceramic was also chosen for the bezel, as it is not subject to wear or loss of colour like anodised aluminium, and it guarantees perfect legibility, even after many years of use. Its immersion scale is in Ceragold or white enamel.

Steel case, waterproof to 30 bar; slightly domed sapphire crystal; screw-in sapphire caseback; screw-down crown; and a screw-down helium escape valve at 10 o'clock, which can also be operated underwater. Unidirectional rotating bezel. Blue ceramic dial with wave pattern; date aperture at 3 o'clock; applied indices with Super-LumiNova inserts; skeletonised hands with Super-LumiNova inserts.

THE 1990S —

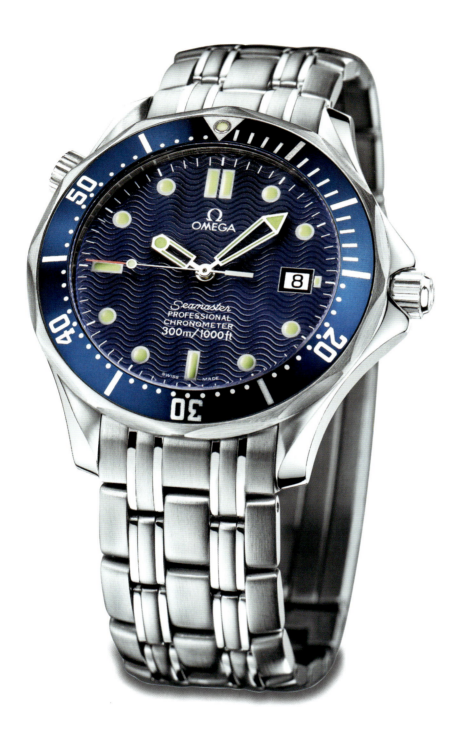

1993

1993

Royal Oak Offshore
Audemars Piguet 1993

At times, if insights arrive too early they can lead to indecision before resulting in a good outcome. This was the case with the Royal Oak Offshore, commissioned by Stephen Urquhart, who was CEO of Audemars Piguet in the late 1980s. He turned to the young designer Emmanuel Gueit and asked him devise a Royal Oak model for a younger audience. The new version was intended to be launched in 1992 for the Royal Oak's twentieth anniversary. Gueit thought it was time to create a chronograph watch of larger proportions. However, as the design developed, the watch appeared to be too massive.

Management decided to wait before it introduced the model, which was revolutionary in the face of an industry offering extra-flat designs. The watch would therefore be released one year later, presented to the market in 1993. The model's presentation caused a stir, and it took a few years for it to achieve success.

What distinguishes this watch from the original Royal Oak is its larger, thicker case due to the movement's insertion into a protective antimagnetic cage, its visible gasket for water resistence, and its weight. The steel version of the first Offshore model weighed 250 grams ($8^{1}/_{5}$ ounces); this rose by 50 grams ($1^{4}/_{5}$ ounces) in the gold edition, and it came to 800 grams ($28^{1}/_{5}$ ounces) in the platinum edition. To set the dial apart while maintaining a connection to the classic model's look, the designers chose to use a "grande tapisserie" pattern, instead of the "petite" version characterising the traditional Royal Oak.

Above all, however, to ensure greater water resistance, the bezel, push-pieces and crown were coated in rubber.

The first Royal Oak Offshore, 1993. The sportier Offshore line still retains the Royal Oak's essential elements.

— THE 1990s

Luminor
Panerai 1993

The Luminor 44mm model was presented in 1993. It quickly became a highly sought-after timepiece, as it evoked important values and a unique, true story through a functional, non-conformist aesthetic. The watch was distinguished by a truly unusual size for its time, coupled with its crown protection bridge, an icon of function-oriented watchmaking. Officine Panerai's first production round of the Luminor 44mm produced 899 examples (reference 5218-201/A) and was entrusted exclusively to important Swiss suppliers. A specific version reserved for the Navy was also prepared in ninety examples, with a blackened anti-reflective, scratch-resistant case (reference 5218-202/A).

The original, unique patented system for the winding crown, using a protective bridge equipped with a locking cam lever, has transformed the Luminor 44mm into a pioneer of world watchmaking trends. The large dimensions of its case and its immediate recognisability have rendered the watch a true reference point for enthusiasts and collectors.

Today Panerai's Luminor 44mm model plays an ever more central role in the Florentine maker's collection. Panerai is continuously searching for new technical solutions and to use innovative materials, including materials that are eco-sustainable and part of a circular economy system, with the aim of protecting the environment (for example, e-Steel). This timepiece therefore continues to testify to the innovative philosophy behind its own creation, devised in Italy and built in Switzerland. The Luminor has become central to the international sports watchmaking scene, past, present and – above all – future.

The Luminor 44mm and Luminor Marina 44mm models' technical features involved a 16-ligne ETA calibre (no. 6497, based on a Unitas calibre), and a 44mm-diameter (1¾in-diameter) AISI 316L stainless-steel case with tested water-resistance up to 400m (1,312ft), guaranteed up to 30 bar.

1993

— THE 1990s

Lange 1
A. Lange & Söhne   1993

The Lange 1 was one of the first watches offered by the A. Lange & Söhne company when it resumed its activities in the early 1990s. This model incorporates some traditional elements of Saxon watchmaking, including a three-quarter plate, screwed gold chatons, and a balance wheel with screws. These build a bridge towards the maker's historical masterpieces, while the patented Outsize Date and off-centre configuration of the dial open a new chapter in the history of the firm's *haute horlogerie*.

This watch was the progenitor of a large family of watches with varying functions and complications, including, for example, the Lange 1 Moon Phase: inspired by Earth's satellite, the Lange masters fitted its moon-phase version with a disc showing a moon in gold that moves continuously, instead of advancing only once or twice a day.

The Lange 1 Time Zone, presented for the first time in 2005, and a white-gold variant with luminous hands and applied indices presented in 2012, allow for a perfect orientation among the twenty-four time zones. This can also be done in the dark, thanks to the rhodium-plated gold luminous hands and indices on both the subsidiary and main dials, displaying the time locally and in another time zone.

In the Lange 1 Tourbillon, a patented stop-seconds mechanism allows the tourbillon to be stopped in order to adjust the watch, with precision to the second. The Lange 1 Tourbillon Perpetual Calendar brings together two classic, refined complications. The self-winding Lange 1 was presented in 2009.

Watch with 38.5mm (1½in) platinum case, silver- and rhodium-plated dial, rhodium-plated gold hands. Calibre L121.1. Alligator strap.

Classique Grande Complication Squelette 3355PT
Breguet 1995

Abraham-Louis Breguet, founder of the Breguet *maison*, made a significant contribution to the development of the watchmaking techniques of his time and would also influence the art of watchmaking in the time to follow. His most famous invention was the tourbillon, patented in 1801, whose purpose was to ensure that a clock ran as smoothly as possible by eliminating the influence of gravity on a watch when positioned vertically.

In its Classique collection, Breguet has interpreted some of the complications through a modern lens. Among them, the tourbillon is one of the most fascinating and attractive, both for the elegance of its design and for its technical innovation.

The Classique line is directly inspired by Breguet's creations. It features the principles that led the great inventor to revolutionise watch design: essential lines, harmony of proportions, and perfect legibility.

The reference 3355PT shows the technical complexities as aesthetic elements, thanks to the skeletonised mechanical movement highlighting its tourbillon mechanism, which can be admired between two sapphire crystals.

The design is enhanced by a semicircular counter, marked to twenty seconds, at 6 o'clock, which is read through the three-pointed seconds hand attached to the tourbillon cage.

The entire movement is finely decorated with engravings.

Classique Grande Complication Squelette, 35mm (1⅜in) platinum case with tourbillon. Hand-wound movement, hand engraved. Small seconds hand on the tourbillon shaft. Compensating balance spring with Breguet overcoil. Chapter ring and seconds semicircle in silvered gold, hand engraved. Waterproof to 30m (90ft).

THE 1990s —

1995

— THE 1990s

Annual Calendar
Patek Philippe 1996

In the spring of 1996, Patek Philippe shocked the world of watchmaking when it presented a new complication, the annual calendar. The year it was launched, the new invention won the Watch of the Year Award in Switzerland. In addition to its aesthetic and technical qualities, the annual calendar offered a complication that was considered "useful", easy to use, and unprecedented.

The annual calendar patented by the manufacturer belongs in the category of "useful complications", positioned between the simple calendar, which must be corrected five times a year following months of less than thirty-one days, and the perpetual calendar, which does not require any kind of adjustment.

A watch with an annual-calendar complication automatically indicates the month, day and date, "recognising" the months consisting of thirty and thirty-one days. It must be adjusted only once a year, on 1 March, by means of the crown. This easy-to-use function, however, requires a complicated mechanism. The Calibre 315 S QA was included in the reference 5035 in yellow gold. Then, the collection evolved and was enhanced with new models; the annual calendar was combined with other complications, such as a power-reserve indicator, or the poetic yet ultra-precise moon-phase complication. The annual calendar was produced in many versions with different dials and stylistic features, from time to time combining various precious materials. Each model, however, must adhere to the guideline that the watch be easily consulted.

White gold case, sapphire crystal caseback, rose dial. Day and month functions, date function in aperture, 24-hour indication, gold applied indices with Roman numerals, alligator strap.

8 Jours
Eberhard & Co. 1997

In 1997, Eberhard & Co. introduced the 8 Jours model. It was the first wristwatch with an 8-day power-reserve indicator, which functioned by means of a special patented device consisting of two overlapping springs, totaling over 1.5 metres (5 feet) in length.

The innovation made it possible to extend the life of the mechanical energy of the watch without causing friction and placing stress on the transmission's teeth and pins. The model was also equipped with an additional indicator showing the amount of power remaining.

In 2008, the *maison* offered a Grande Taille edition of the 8 Jours, with a 41-millimetre (1⅗-inch) case diameter. Additionally, so the magic of its movement could be admired, the 8 Jours Grande Taille featured a porthole on its caseback, protected by sapphire crystal. This allows a glimpse of the bridge of its large skeleton barrel, with its silhouetted figure "8". The "8" shows off the oeil-de-perdrix finish on its underside, and the resulting three-dimensional vision offers a glimpse of the second, exceptionally long spring.

Manual-wind mechanical watch with 41mm (1⅗in) steel, a white dial with applied Roman numerals, leaf hands, small seconds at 6 o'clock, a power reserve indicator at 9 o'clock, and crocodile bracelet. Eight-day power reserve. Exclusive item by Eberhard & Co.

Aquanaut
Patek Philippe 1997

In 1997, Patek Philippe introduced the Aquanaut collection, reinterpreting the Nautilus without distorting it. The new watch, inspired by the shape of ocean liner portholes like its predecessor, met the expectations of a young clientele, fond of classic values but also animated by a passion for the modern. Its case was waterproof up to 120 metres (393 feet), guaranteed a high level of safety by its screw-down crown and Tropical straps; these were made of a non-irritating composite material that was ultra-resistant to salt water, traction and ultraviolet rays.

The black dial and strap featured a squared pattern, which was nicknamed "chocolate bar".

The 38.8-millimetre (1½-inch) case with a steel bracelet was introduced in 1998; and in 1999 Patek Philippe presented the same model in yellow gold. In 2007, the collection celebrated its ten-year run with a men's model, available in two large sizes: 38.8 millimetre (1½ inch) and 40.8 millimetre (1⅗ inch). The polished octagonal case retained its shape, and its dial and bracelet adopted the Aquanaut's unmistakable style for the first time.

With its sporty character, the Aquanaut model's first reference (5060A) was initially launched in stainless steel, and multiple variations would follow over the years: in yellow or pink gold, with diamond-set cases, and with dials and bands available in green, blue or white. In 2011, the Aquanaut housed its first Travel Time complication. A skeletonised hour hand indicated the time in a second time zone. To ease its interpretation, two windows were added where a colour change indicated daytime and night-time in the two time zones.

Watch with 35.6mm (1⅖in) steel case, bracelet made of hypoallergenic material, black dial with date window at 3 o'clock, Arabic indices, and luminescent white gold hands.

Léman Tourbillon Automatic (reference 2125-1527-53)
Blancpain 1998

The tourbillon is a device that improves the accuracy of mechanical watches, compensating, thanks to its continual change of position, for the effects of gravity on the function of the watch. It is built as a rotating cage enclosing the balance wheel and balance spring, the escapement wheel, and the anchor. This cage is usually connected to the seconds wheel, and this drives it. Because the seconds wheel typically turns 360 degrees per minute, the tourbillon also makes a full rotation every 60 seconds. This rotation compensates for deviations due to gravity and ensures the highest possible accuracy. Conceived in the late eighteenth century, this system was created for pocket watches, which were manually wound. This is the reason why, when it was first housed in wristwatches, the tourbillon was associated with manually wound movements.

In 1998, Blancpain released the Calibre 25, the first self-winding tourbillon movement with an 8-day power reserve.

Blancpain's automatic Léman Tourbillon was one of the first watches to be powered by the Calibre 25. From an aesthetic perspective, the model reflects the canons of Blancpain's classic *haute horlogerie*, oriented towards a purity of line. The white dial is interrupted at 12 o'clock to reveal the tourbillon's cage, and a power-reserve indicator appears at 6 o'clock.

Automatic watch with tourbillon and 8-day power reserve, 38mm (1½in) white gold case, white dial, applied indices and skeletonised hands, with a crocodile strap.

THE 1990s

1998

— THE 1990s

Tourbillon with Three Gold Bridges
Girard-Perregaux 1999

Around the year 1860, Constant Girard created a pocket watch with a tourbillon movement that had three parallel nickel bridges, which greatly improved the accuracy of the timepiece. In his later creations, gold was used as a functional material, and the structure of the bridges was refined. Its architecture was the result of many years of development, and of a completely innovative vision: the movement was no longer just a technical, functional component but had become a design element in its own right. Thus, the *Tourbillon sous trois ponts d'or* (Tourbillon with Three Gold Bridges) was born in 1889.

At the end of the 1970s, amid the crisis in the Swiss watch industry, Girard-Perregaux decided to make twenty pocket watches matching the 1889 original. In 1991, the maker achieved a new feat when it produced a miniaturised version of the Tourbillon, small enough for a wristwatch.

The shape of the wrist tourbillon would evolve in the years that followed, featuring thinner bridges and a skeletonised edition. The manufacture also developed an inverted construction of the movement, with the bridges facing its caseback, in order to offer models with a dial and equip the Tourbillon with various complications – specifically, to design a model with a chronograph and perpetual calendar. In 1999, Girard-Perregaux launched a self-winding version of the Tourbillon with Three Gold Bridges. In recent years, elegant and ingenious innovations have fuelled a large collection that is continuously evolving.

Watch with 41mm (1⅗in) round pink-gold case. Its functions are hours and minutes, with small seconds on the tourbillon. The strap is alligator with a pink-gold folding clasp.

The 2000s

New Paths of Luxury

The world changed very quickly with the start of the new millennium, especially thanks to technology. The spread of the iPhone and iPad have forever changed people's relationship with communication, shopping and the media, which has also influenced the aesthetics of objects. The iPhone is not only a technological tool, it has also become an icon. Demand for personalised luxury also emerged in this social context, with tailor-made solutions. Innovative technologies that could be exploited to respond to aesthetic and functional tastes, and the trend towards a re-reading of products' histories, characterised not only the design, but many other aspects of consumption.

Fashion was again the emblem of luxury and refinement. There was a reinterpretation of the elegant but comfortable style of the fifties, especially in men's fashion. The truly innovative aspect of it was the exploration of shapes and different combinations, leading to a touch of refinement being added to everything casual, and sportswear elements added to evening wear, merging into a new look that blended classic and high-tech elements, with the inclusion of precious or glamorous details like satin lapels, lamé fabric details, or velvet jackets. Watch design also followed this trend, with cases of grand dimensions and great attention paid to materials and colour combinations: the yellow, pink or white gold in bracelets and cases was combined with mother-of-pearl or enamel dials in a variety of colours, from the subtlest to the most vivid.

Identity and Heritage

Watches belong to the luxury sector, a sector that underwent enormous changes at the beginning of the new millennium. Branding became crucial.

◀ *George Clooney, representing the refined elegance of the 2000s. He is wearing an Omega Seamaster Aqua Terra.*

Since 2000, each brand has positioned its product very clearly within a pyramid of luxury consumption, at the top of which sits bespoke luxury, characterised by unique pieces made by hand and offered according to a strategy based on inaccessibility. The second group in the pyramid contains luxury products that are manufactured in limited editions and sold at a select number of outlets. Finally, at the base of the pyramid sit everyday luxury items, or products that maintain a high level of quality, but are offered on the market at a price that allows for them to be purchased by a greater number of consumers.[1] Price therefore became a fundamental variable in defining the positioning of a company's system of distribution, but not price alone: it was equally important to define what is termed "brand identity". Identity is something rooted in the brand's history and is the result of a unique, inimitable historical journey. Just consider the ways in which a distant tradition is referenced in fine watchmaking, considered indispensable in legitimising a company's belonging to the sector. For example, the company Vacheron Constantin's communications campaign in 2010 centred on a portrayal of a document being signed at the company's incorporation in Geneva, 1755. In this case, the use of history was intended to involve the consumer emotionally and affirm the brand's authenticity through its heritage. In addition to this, makers understood the importance of "style identity": that is, an aesthetic language that continuously distinguishes a company's products despite those products being regularly updated over time. Communication has occupied an increasingly central role since the beginning of the millennium, when companies had to deal with a highly articulated world of consumption and were forced to define their voices ever more distinctly. This is because digital consumers of this era desire strong involvement with a brand, one with which they share values. Watchmaking houses have therefore begun to carefully select endorsements, ambassadors, green projects, sports sponsorships, charity events, and forms of support for the arts which align with the values of the brand.

The entry of many Swiss manufacturers into large luxury groups including LVMH, Richemont, Kering and Swatch has favoured the implementation of well-defined marketing activities. However, independent companies have also worked to clearly define their own identities.

AESTHETICS AND FUNCTIONALITY

Their success in the watch market sector prompted the Bulgari Group to launch a vertical integration strategy with the aim of increasing its expertise in the watchmaking sector, achieving the highest quality standards and optimising production processes.

Confirming the importance that the high-end watchmaking market assumed in the brand's history, in 2000, the Bulgari Group acquired the two leading brands that produced high-end Swiss watches, Daniel Roth and Gérald Genta. In 2005, it acquired Swiss companies Cadrans Design, which was active in the production of high-end watch dials, and Prestige d'Or, leader in the production of steel and precious-metal bracelets. Finally, in 2007, the Swiss company Finger,

---

[1] CAPPELLARI, ROMANO, *Marketing della moda e dei prodotti lifestyle*, Carocci Editore, Rome 2016, p. 92.

specialising in the production of sophisticated cases for complicated watches, and Leschot, which produces watch components to support the development of a new movement's manufacture, also joined the Bulgari Group. With these acquisitions, Bulgari created the first complicated, limited-edition movement, entirely conceived, produced and assembled within the group. In 2009, for its 125th anniversary, Bulgari released the Sotirio Bulgari collection, with in-house movements comprising a perpetual calendar movement with tourbillon, an annual calendar, an automatic movement with the date, and a movement with a retrograde date display. In 2010, the first Bulgari base calibre was born. In the same year, seven new watches revisited the characteristic models of its two *maisons*, preserving all the technical and aesthetic characteristics of their creations. The Bulgari Daniel Roth collection revisited the Tourbillon Rattrapante, Endurer Chronosprint and Tourbillon Lumière, while revisited Gérald Genta models included the Octo Chronographe Quadri-Retro, the Octo Répétition Minutes Retro, and, most especially, the Octo Grande Sonnerie Tourbillon. In these watches, the Bulgari logo appeared on the dial together with those of Daniel Roth and Gérald Genta. In 2012, the Bulgari brand introduced its Octo model, destined to become an icon of the fashion house.

In these years, the Cartier *maison* explored the traditional shape of the watch by introducing, in 2009, the Ballon Bleu model. It had a circular case and simple outline, yet it played with proportions and was characterised by a winding crown formed by a blue sphere with integrated crown cover, protected by a metal arch at 3 o'clock. It would become one of the maker's top models, distinguishing itself as a unisex watch.

Ballon Bleu de Cartier wristwatch with automatic movement, 42mm (1$^7/_{10}$in). Cartier, 2009. Steel, one blue spinel cabochon. Round movement, automatic, date, Côtes de Genève decoration, rhodium-plated, 21 jewels, shockproof, anchor escapement, monometallic balance wheel, flat hairspring. Case measuring 4.37 x 4.4 x 1.3cm (1$^7/_{10}$ x 1$^7/_{10}$ x ½in), including lugs and crown.

In 2001, Eberhard & Co. introduced an interpretation of time that was completely unique in the field of chronographs: the Chrono 4 was the first and only chronograph in the history of watchmaking with four counters arranged horizontally in a linear progression, showing the minutes, hours, 24-hour clock, and small seconds in succession.

To crown more than a century of professional excellence, in 1999, Breitling decided to produce chronometers exclusively, subjecting all its production to the tests of the Contrôle officiel suisse des chronomètres (COSC). Since then, all Breitling watches have obtained the official chronometer qualification. In 2009, Breitling introduced its Calibre 01, a chronograph movement designed for the greatest possible regularity, which uses a column wheel and offers a power reserve of over 70 hours, entirely designed and manufactured in the maker's laboratories.

Continuing to cultivate the art of *haute horlogerie*, in the new millennium Girard-Perregaux presented reinterpretations of some of its most emblematic watches, the Laureato Evo3 Tourbillon, with three sapphire bridges (2006) and the Vintage 1945 Jackpot Tourbillon (2007) being two examples. The maker also claimed numerous world firsts, including a combined perpetual calendar and world timer (2006) and a chronograph Tourbillon with split-seconds and Foudroyante (or "jumping seconds") functions (2008).

Rolex, on the other hand, made use of interest in its vintage sports models, the Submariner, the GMT and the Daytona, offering them in versions with revised shapes and designs, and demand for them quickly exceeded supply. In 2003, the Submariner with a green bezel, nicknamed "Kermit", was introduced to celebrate the fiftieth anniversary of the model. In 2005, again as a celebratory model for its fiftieth anniversary, the GMT with a ceramic bezel was introduced. In 2007, a new version of the Milgauss was introduced at the Basel fair: this model retained its antimagnetic qualities and presented new features, like its 40-millimetre ($1^3/_5$-inch) case, a polished finish, and a dial available in black and white.

Appreciation of Heritage

From a heritage perspective, it is always important to recount and appreciate a maker's history; but it is equally fundamental to preserve and interpret the technical tradition of a *maison* according to a contemporary lexicon. Such is the case of Breguet, heir to a rich history of watchmaking, whose horologists have practised, and continue to practise, their craft. This is especially true in the complications sector, where the maker has continued to demonstrate its creative capacity and celebrate its history at the same time. The Tourbillon Messidor, for example, was introduced in 2001 to celebrate the 200-year patent of the tourbillon by Abraham-Louis Breguet. In 2006, the Double Tourbillon was introduced, with a two-tourbillon system visible on its dial. With the Classique collection, the *maison* continues to elaborate on its founder's timeless horological practices in the context of contemporary horology. Its historical Marine collection and Type XXII model have also been reinterpreted, with new offerings in both technology and materials.

A reinterpretation of old traditions led to the Jaquet Droz workshop's recovery of its own creative codes, elaborated and refined over time since its establishment in 1738 by master watchmaker Pierre Jaquet-Droz.

Longines also participated in strategic development through the company's historical heritage. In 2002, to celebrate the 170th anniversary of the *maison*, the maker introduced Les Elégantes, a collection of three vintage models echoing 1930s design. In addition to timelessly elegant watches, today Longines chiefly cultivates the legacy of its models related to the world of aviation, including the Longines Spirit collection. Professional timekeeping, an important pillar of Longines to this day, is reflected in the new model of the Ultra-Chron: this watch, with an exceptionally precise, high-frequency movement (5Hz) references the first high-frequency chronometers. Longines launched the first chronometer capable of measuring to 1/10 of a second as early as 1914 and another, even more accurate, in 1916, which displayed the time elapsed to 1/100 of a second. This pioneering spirit lives on in its new collections.

By joining the Swatch group in 2000, the Glashütte Original brand was able to satisfy the technological and financial conditions necessary to guarantee its brand-creative autonomy and production flexibility. In the 2000s, the maker outlined its offerings, defining its various lines: Art & Technik, which creates models with complications, the Pano collection models, Senator Diary, and Senator Perpetual Calendar; the Quintessentials line, which includes models representing the essence of the maker's watchmaking art, including the Senator collection; the Twentieth Century Vintage line, conveying attention to design; and its Sixties and Seventies collections; meanwhile, the watches in its Navigator series reference the pilot watches it produced in the interwar years.

The promotion of the Blancpain maker's own history was combined with cutting-edge technological development, which in 2008 introduced the Carrousel Volant Une Minute, a complication forgotten for over a century which the *maison* incorporated into a wristwatch for the first time. This is the first complication in which the cage makes a complete revolution in one minute. Drawing on the watchmaker's rich history,

In 2005, on the 250th anniversary of its foundation, Vacheron Constantin created the Tour de l'Ile, made in only seven examples, which features 16 watch complications and astronomical indications.

the company's new management reinterpreted the collections to express the brand's most representative values, relaunching the Fifty Fathoms and revising the Villeret collection from a contemporary perspective.

Innovation and Tradition

Aware of the historical value of its brand, Officine Panerai has continued with the concept of watches inspired by models once intended for military use, capable of meeting extremely high technical requirements. Officine Panerai's present and future operate through the in-house development of high-quality manufacturing movements and the search for innovative materials. The Radiomir was offered in Tourbillon and Chronograph editions, and in 2004 the Radiomir 45mm Black Seal, Radiomir 8 Days and Radiomir GMT were born. The Luminor, distinguished by its characteristic patented crown-protecting bridge design to ensure water resistance, was offered as a "time-only" model or with complications, including chronograph, GMT and power reserve models. The collection presented in 2012 used only in-house movements and excellent, high-performance materials: stainless steel, ceramic and, for the first time, red gold. The beginning of the new millennium was marked by a fusion of tradition with modernity, due to the company's maturation in the field of high-end watchmaking and its numerous reinterpretations of this early art's characteristic elements.

Of the watches produced by Jaeger-LeCoultre in the new millennium, the Reverso Quantième Perpètuel and the Master Grande Memovox are standouts, alongside the Reverso Platinum Number One, the first Reverso in platinum to feature the watchmaker's first fully skeletonised manual calibre. In 2004, it introduced the Gyrotourbillon, a spherical tourbillon of memorable complications. In 2006, Jaeger-LeCoultre brought together the measurement of civil time, sidereal time and astral time in a single watch: the Reverso Grande Complication à Triptyque was born, with three main dials to read three visions of time. The Duomètre collection, which was born in 2007, introduced the Dual-Wing concept, new to watchmaking design. With the Dual-Wing concept, the horologists at the Jaeger-LeCoultre workshop have developed a solution that provides an answer to a recurring problem in complex mechanical watches: that complications use some of the energy provided by the barrel. A Dual-Wing design allows for the separation of the energy needed to power the complication from the energy of the watch movement, powered by its barrel, to ensure a constant supply. This movement allowed Jaeger-LeCoultre to bring the accuracy of the Duomètre Chronographe to the level of a chronometer's, measuring time with an accuracy to within 1/6 of a second. It then found a new application in the Duomètre Quantième Lunaire and the Duomètre Sphérotourbillon.

Historical collections were also renewed at Vacheron Constantin in the early 2000s. In its Malte collection, the *maison* took up the tonneau-shaped models that had characterised the maker's production in the early twentieth century, while the Patrimony line, with a classic shape, offered space for complications, and the Historiques collection reproduces historical pieces using new techniques. Vacheron Constantin turned to customisation with the Quai de l'Ile line, which, thanks to the modular construction of the case, allows for the creation of customised watches based on a series of parameters. It was through its Atelier Cabinotiers, however, that the maker decided to convey the concept of exclusivity. Returning to the philosophy of the *cabinotiers*, cultured and refined master watchmakers – part-artists, part-philosophers – with the Atelier Cabinotiers Special Order service (established by Vacheron Constantin in 2006), the atelier offers its customers a very exclusive service: to create one-of-a-kind, completely bespoke timepieces.

IWC also reinforced the strong link with its technical and aesthetic work from the past. In 1993, the Schaffhausen-based *maison* had already relaunched the Portugieser. Sixty years following its conception, the new Portuguese was an imposing watch of remarkably large dimensions for the 1990s, made of steel, red gold, or platinum, and distinguished by its large, inimitable dial, rendered all the more prominent by its very thin bezel. To place the right emphasis on its refined mechanics, it was also given a sapphire crystal caseback. The result was surprising: not only were all 1,750 watches constructed (1,000 in steel, 500 in red gold, and 250 in platinum) sold in a short period of time, but the Portuguese helped to launch a fashion for large watches. In 2005, the Ingenieur, one of IWC's most famous models, was celebrated fifty years after it was first presented, with the introduction of an automatic and a chronograph version. The new generation is perfectly resistant to shocks, bumps and vibrations, and it works reliably despite the widespread magnetism emitted by an increasing number of machines and appliances surrounding us on a daily basis. In 2006, there was the relaunch of the Pilot's Watch line, and the Da Vinci line, which included several models with complications, debuted the following year. The Big Ingenieur, with a 45.5-millimetre (1¾-inch) steel case, met notable success in 2007. In 2008, for the 140th anniversary of its founding, IWC celebrated its six legendary watch family "founders" with an exclusive IWC Vintage Collection. In 2009, the AquaTimer, Portugieser, Portofino and Pilot's Watch families were renewed.

The Saxon company A. Lange & Söhne, which became part of the Richemont Group, continued with the creation of new models: the Langematik Perpetual, introduced in 2001; the Lange 1 Moon Phase, launched in 2002; the Lange Double Split manual flyback chronograph, presented in 2004; and the innovative Lange Zeitwerk in 2009. All these models referenced the maker's traditional stylistic codes, yet inserted important technical innovations. With the presentation of the

Zeitwerk watch by A. Lange & Söhne with 42mm (1⁷⁄₁₀in) white gold case, silvered dial, hours and minutes with "jumping" digits, indication of the power reserve.

Zeitwerk in 2009, A. Lange & Söhne ushered in a new era of timekeeping. The characteristic face and the innovative concept of the first mechanical wristwatch with a digital time indication, showing the hours and minutes using jumping digits, fascinated enthusiasts. This project took on the time display of the monumental clocks typically used in theatres. In 2010, the Homage to F.A. Lange was introduced in celebration of the maker's 165th anniversary; it included three timepieces produced in limited series: the Tourbograph "Pour le Mérite", the Lange 1 Tourbillon with a tourbillon and stop-seconds function (a Lange patent), and the 1815 Moon Phase.

Made in 2005 for the "Only Watch" charity auction, organised by Antiquorum in Montecarlo, the "DBS" by De Bethune represents the excellent combination of technical savoir-faire and contemporary aesthetic qualities.

Bold and Innovative

The late 1990s and early 2000s saw the resurgence of independent watchmaking, with the appearance of brands such as Roger Dubuis, Richard Mille and De Bethune. These began to create bold, experimental watches that challenged the aesthetics of conventional watchmaking while also using innovative materials, such as titanium and carbon.

Experiments at extremely high technical levels were also taking place at well-established historical watchmakers such as Patek Philippe, which with the beginning of the new millennium presented a series of exceptional models in the technique of watchmaking. The Star Caliber, a pocket watch produced in 2000, required eight years of study and research to create. With the twenty-one complications enclosed in its savonnette case, it was the third most complicated watch in the world; moreover, six of its twenty-one complications were absolute novelties patented by Patek Philippe. The 2001 Sky Moon Tourbillon was the most complicated wristwatch produced by Patek Philippe, followed in 2005 by the thinnest single-button split-seconds chronograph ever created, and in 2006, the chronograph with an annual calendar. With the beginning of the new millennium, Patek Philippe devoted itself to revisiting historical models: for example, the Gondolo of the 1920s, both with an oval and cushion-shaped case. The *maison* also redesigned another iconic model, the Calatrava, the epitome of classic style, into a more contemporary format. In recent years, the maker's focus was honed in other areas as well. The company philosophy observes the life of a watch over time, and the company guarantees its quality over the years. In 2009, the maker introduced the Patek Philippe Seal, which certifies the entire manufacturing control system, from the materials used to the individual structural elements.

In 2000, Audemars Piguet grappled with the rare time equation complication. This complication takes into account the fact that the duration of the solar day is not constant over the course of the year due to the elliptical shape of the Earth's orbit, while the measurement of conventional time is based on a day of constant duration, the average day. The difference between solar time and mean time is called the equation of time. Watches equipped with this complication have two hands: one that indicates the conventional time, the other that marks the solar time, allowing for the difference between the two to be read. The Jules Audemars Equation of Time was born on this technological basis, also equipped with a perpetual calendar and lunar phases, even indicating the time of sunrise and sunset. In 2002, technical, ultra-modern precision met state-of-the-art micromechanics in the Royal Oak Concept, which has since offered a platform for Audemars Piguet experimentation. The new millennium is also witnessing continued experimentation in the field of materials, with the use of carbon for the 2008 Royal Oak Offshore Carbon Concept Tourbillon.

Technical Renewal

In 1999, Omega introduced an important technical innovation: it was the Omega Co-Axial Calibre 2500, equipped with the Co-Axial escapement, developed in collaboration with the watchmaker George Daniels. This escapement significantly limited the friction that arose between parts making up the watch, requiring less maintenance and, above all, ensuring greater stability of the watch's accuracy in the long run. The consequent reduction in friction made virtually any lubricant superfluous, minimising the need for maintenance in Co-Axial calibres. In the ten years that followed the launch of the first Co-Axial calibre, Omega introduced the innovative escapement in all its watch lines, with top-level chronometric performance, thus also making them available for mechanical watches manufactured on an industrial scale. In 2007, Omega presented the Co-Axial Calibre 8500, entirely developed and manufactured in-house by the *maison*. The adventure continued in 2008 with the Co-Axial Calibre 8520/8521, specially designed for smaller watches, and the Co-Axial Calibre 8601/8611, a movement with annual calendar indications that update with an instantaneous click. Also in 2008, the introduction of the Silicon balance spring to these new co-axial in-house calibres lengthened the warranty of each individual watch to four years.

An Apparent Paradox

The history of wristwatches began with a technical challenge: to build them smaller than pocket watches, but without losing reliability and precision. Today, however, technology is part of our life. Around the world, there are now billions of messages sent daily, and we all transmit just as many videos, like electronic postcards, to stimulate the thoughts, memories and curiosity of others. We use the computer as a professional tool; but now, also for entertainment and updates. To find out about stock-market trends, or read the latest news, we can connect to the internet from anywhere: hotels, offices or convention centres. To check our appointments, we consult an electronic calendar. Strictly speaking, no one needs to wear a watch to know what time it is; multiple digital tools tell us the time. Yet, despite having to deal with digital tools, the exclusive charm of mechanical movements wins out.

This is a paradox of the watch industry: if the watch seems to have lost its primary function, it still maintains its role as a luxury accessory. In addition to being a reflection of style and taste, what you wear on your wrist is a significant sign of character.

Iconic models are among the modern objects of desire. A mechanical watch embodies the magic of a technical knowledge that still fascinates humankind. It represents an intrinsic value, and an intangible value linked to the prestige of owning an object adored for its form and design. It is not simply a question of luxury as a status symbol, but as a search for creative and cultural excellence.

— THE 2000s

PanoRetroGraph
Glashütte Original   2000

In 2000, Glashütte Original presented its PanoRetroGraph at the Basel Fair. This example of high-end German watchmaking had such an innovative design that, in 2001, it was awarded the Watch of the Year Award. The development of the PanoRetroGraph has written a new chapter in the history of horology. Unlike other conventional wrist chronographs, which have the function of measuring time only as it progresses, this watch is capable of measuring time both forwards and backwards. This option is made possible by a complex reverse gear that removes potential inaccuracies. The crown allows for countdowns to be set up to a maximum interval of thirty minutes.

The function also features audible chimes when the preselected countdown time has expired. This explains the term "Retro" that makes up part of its name, while "Pano" refers to the large date display, and "Graph" corresponds to its chronograph function.

Twelve years later, at the Baselworld International Watch Show in 2012, a new version of the Pano models was presented, featuring a cylindrical case of the same diameter as the previous one, but surrounded by a thinner bezel. Its new proportions offered a more spacious dial. The 2012 models also featured the typical elements of their predecessors: a decentralised arrangement of hours, minutes and small seconds, with a large panoramic date.

Platinum case with sapphire crystal caseback, gold base dial with hand-made guilloché decoration. The hour display is off-centre, on the left side, and intersected by that of the small seconds, while the Panorama Date, hallmark of the maison, *is at 4 o'clock. The chronograph seconds counter with cumulative scales is positioned at 2 o'clock. Crocodile strap.*

Sky Moon Tourbillon
Patek Philippe   2001

Introduced in 2001, the Sky Moon Tourbillon reference 5002 was the most complicated wristwatch that Patek Philippe produced and the first double-faced wristwatch in the history of the maker.

This creation showed several complicated yet fascinating aspects of timekeeping. On the dial side, it features a complete perpetual calendar, with a date indication via a retrograde hand from 2 to 10 o'clock, while four subsidiary dials by means of their hands indicate the day of the week, the month, the leap-year cycle, and the age of the Moon. On the caseback side, one can admire a celestial map of the northern hemisphere, with moon phases, moon orbit display, and sidereal time. Complications of this watch include a minute repeater and tourbillon.

For the technicians and master watchmakers of the Geneva-based maker, inserting twelve complications in the small space of a wristwatch was a true challenge and a further step towards absolute miniaturisation. The manual winding movement of this masterpiece is in fact made up of 686 components, some of which are microscopic in size.

In 2013, Patek Philippe gave the Sky Moon Tourbillon a new look with the reference 6002, which, unlike the 5002, indicates the moon phase rather than the moon age and has apertures instead of hands to display the day of the week, month and leap year. The main differences, however, are found in its aesthetics. The double-sided case, crowns, slider, hour and minute hands, and folding clasp are decorated with entirely hand-engraved scrolls and arabesques. The front of the dial combines grand feu champlevé and cloisonné enamel.

Sky Moon Tourbillon reference 5002 with platinum case, not waterproof. Front: perpetual calendar with retrograde date hand, mean solar time (daylight saving time) hours and minutes, day, month, leap year with hand, age of the Moon. Back: sidereal hour, sky chart, lunar phases and angular movement of the moon on the night sky background. Hand-wound mechanical movement. Functions: minute repeater, tourbillon. Two-tone "cathedral" gongs, operated by a slider integrated with the case. Alligator strap.

2001

… THE 2000s —

Chrono 4
Eberhard & Co.   2001

In 2001 Eberhard & Co. presented a collection that represented a revolution in the chronograph sector, both technically and aesthetically. In fact, for the first time ever in the history of watchmaking, all the chronograph counters and subsidiary dials were arranged horizontally on the dial and no longer stationed radially in the usual positions, i.e., at 3, 6, 9 or 12 o'clock. The innovation introduced by the *maison* was not only a great example of technical research and development, but also a new way to read the time. With the registers aligned, the reading was much more immediate, because the calculation took place according to a natural sequence: first the minutes elapsed since the start of timing, then the hours, all in succession and with an evident logic, without having to identify the various counters and related indications on the dial. From a technical point of view, the device, patented by Eberhard & Co., involved a considerable complexity of construction, considering, for example, that the mechanical functionality of the movement made use of 53 jewels. Equal attention was also paid to the search for aesthetic details, especially with exquisite care taken with the case, back and dial.

Chronograph with 4mm (⅛in) case. The dial is white with black counters. The date window is at 12 o'clock, while the tachymeter scale for calculating speed is placed outside the indices, which are topped with a dot of lume, as are its dagger-shaped hands. Crocodile strap.

Royal Oak Concept
Audemars Piguet 2002

In 2002, to celebrate the thirtieth anniversary of the Royal Oak, Audemars Piguet introduced the Royal Oak Concept, a model made with materials previously unheard of in watchmaking. The creative director of the manufacture, Claude Emmenegger, was inspired by concept cars when selecting them. The case was made of alacrite 602, an alloy of chromium and tungsten with a high percentage of cobalt; it is very resistant, though difficult to work. Its mainplate (the supporting structure of the movement, to which all the wheels are fixed, the jewels are fitted, and bridges are secured) was made of titanium. The movement housed a tourbillon, a dynamograph, and power reserve indicator. For the first time, the Royal Oak was offered with a Kevlar strap, highlighting its sporty spirit.

Audemars Piguet's collaboration with the Alinghi sailing team allowed the maker to broaden its research horizons towards materials that were unusual for watchmaking but typical of other sectors, such as sailing. The Royal Oak Concept Carbon emerged from the workshops of the Le Brassus *maison* in 2008, made of forged carbon, a resistant, light and malleable material. Machined to extremely fine fibres, the forged carbon is combined with complementary materials such as ceramic or titanium to obtain interesting shades. Produced in only 150 examples, this model, however, was an interesting experiment, and the starting point for the development of future carbon watches.

Royal Oak Concept, alacrite 602 case and caseback, 44mm (1¾in) diameter, titanium bezel, dial composed of mainplate, raised minute track with hour markers. Indications: hours, minutes, power reserve (calibrated in the number of barrel turns), function selector with additional push-piece and function indicator, tourbillon at 9 o'clock and dynamograph display at 12 o'clock. Kevlar strap.

THE 2000s —

2002

— THE 2000s

DE VECCHI, PAOLO and ALBERTO UGLIETTI. *Wristwatches: The Models that Made an Age*. Novara: De Agostini, 2014.

EMCH, MANUEL. *Jaquet Droz*. New York: Assouline, 2010.

FRITZ, MANFRED AND PAULO COELHO. *IWC: Engineering Time Since 1868*. Schaffhausen: IWC Schaffhausen, 2010.

GAUTIER, GILBERTE. *Cartier the Legend*. London: Arlington Books, 1983.

GENOUD, HERVÈ, *Breitling: The Book*. La Chaux-de-Fonds: Breitling, 2009.

GOLDBERGER, JOHN AND GIAMPIERO NEGRETTI. *Longines Watches*. Bologna: Damiani, 2006.

HUBER, MARTIN AND ALAN BANBERY. *Patek Philippe Genève*. Geneva: Antiquorum, 1988.

LANDES, DAVID S. *Revolution in Time: Clocks and the Making of the Modern World*. Cambridge, Mass.: Belknap Press of Harvard University Press, 1983.

MARINETTI, FILIPPO TOMMASO. *Come si seducono le donne e si tradiscono gli uomini*, in Pautasso, Guido Andrea, ed. "Moda Futurista. Eleganza e seduzione", Milan: Abscondita, 2016.

MAROZZI, DARIA AND GIANLUIGI TOSELLI. *Longines*. Bologna: Giada Edizioni, 1990.

MEIS, REINHARD. *A. Lange & Söhne: The Watchmakers of Dresden*. Geneva: Antiquorum Editions, 1999.

NADELHOFFER, HANS. *Cartier: Jewelers Extraordinary*. London: Thames and Hudson, 1984.

NEGRETTI, GIAMPIERO AND SIMON DE BURTON. *Panerai*. Paris: Éditions Flammarion, 2008.

PATRIZZI, OSVALDO. *Cartier Bianco/White Cartier*. Milan: Patrizzi & Co. Editions, 2011.

———. *Collezionare orologi da polso Rolex/Collecting Rolex Wristwatches*. Milan: Guido Mondani Editore, 2011.

PATRIZZI, OSVALDO AND MADELEINE PATRIZZI. *Collezionare orologi da polso Patek Philippe/Collecting Patek Philippe Watches*. Milan: Guido Mondani Editore, 2004.

PATRIZZI, OSVALDO AND MARA CAPPELLETTI. *Investing in Wristwatches: Rolex*. Woodbridge: ACC Art Books, 2021.

———. *Rolex: History, Icons and Record-Breaking Models*. Woodbridge: Antique Collectors' Club, 2015.

———. "Patek Philippe: Il lusso discreto delle complicazioni". Milan: 24 Ore Cultura, 2013.

RAULET, SYLVIE. *Art Deco Jewelry*. New York: Rizzoli International Publications, 1985.

SCARPELLINI, EMANUELA. *Material Nation: A Consumer's History of Modern Italy*. New York: Oxford University Press, 2011.

All notes on men's fashion are taken from lessons from "Moda maschile dal 1900 al 2000" (Men's Fashion from 1900 to 2000) by Massimo Borgia, founder of the Eduna school for continuing education.

PHOTO CREDITS

pp. 4, 252: © Glashütte Original

pp. 6, 59, 71, 82, 83, 118, 126, 127, 140, 143, 148, 162, 164, 186, 215: © Rolex

pp. 9, 62, 63, 66, 91, 113, 152, 171, 190, 199, 232, 236, 255: © Patek Philippe

pp. 10, 97, 109, 147, 168: © Archivio storico IWC Schaffhausen

pp. 12, 79, 92, 136, 151, 160, 181, 184, 223: © Omega

pp. 14, 104, 110, 111, 227: © Panerai

pp. 16, 27, 33, 159, 189, 217, 224, 259: © Audemars Piguet

p. 18: © Getty Images / Hulton Archive

p. 20: © Getty Images / Print Collector

pp. 21, 39, 178, 240: © Girard-Perregaux

p. 22: WikiCommons / John T. Daniels

p. 25: Cartier Paris Documentation © Paul Tissandier

pp. 26, 43, 58, 101, 106, 129, 235: © Archivi storici Eberhard & Co.

pp. 29, 37, 41, 47, 56, 65, 81, 84, 87, 105, 107, 114, 124, 125, 157, 158, 163, 172, 180, 183: Courtesy of Sotheby's

pp. 30, 205, 212: Marian Gérard, Cartier Collection © Cartier

p. 31: Cartier Paris Archives © Cartier

p. 34: © Getty Images / W. G. Phillips

pp. 38, 51, 167, 198: Vincent Wulveryck, Cartier Collection © Cartier

pp. 40, 45: WikiCommons

p. 42: WikiCommons / Sergei Gutnikov

p. 44: © Museo Francesco Baracca Lugo

p. 48: © Archivio storico Breitling

p. 52: © Getty Images / Underwood Archives

p. 55: Nils Herrmann, Cartier Collection © Cartier

pp. 57, 80, 102, 117, 256: © Eberhard & Co. photo Stefano Campo Antico

pp. 60, 61, 72, 73: © Archivio storico Longines Watch Company Francillon

p. 69: © Antiquorum Genève SA

p. 74: © Getty Images / Bettmann

pp. 77, 88, 89, 122, 132, 162, 260: © Jaeger-LeCoultre

pp. 94, 231, 263: © Collection Montres Breguet

p. 98: © Alamy Foto Stock / Glasshouse Images

p. 120: © Getty Images / Archive Photos

p. 128: Courtesy of Jaeger-LeCoultre © Johann SAUTY

pp. 130, 139, 206, 209, 239: © Blancpain

p. 135: © Archivio storico Breitling

p. 144: © Phillips

p. 154: © Getty Images / Keystone

p. 174: © Getty Images / Popperfoto, Rolls Press

p. 177: © Seiko

p. 182: © Movado

pp. 193, 264: Courtesy of Bulgari

p. 194: © Alamy Foto Stock / Ronald Grant Archive, 20th CENTURY FOX

pp. 196, 202, 213, 214, 220: © Swatch Ltd

p. 210: © Getty Images / Keith Hamshere

pp. 219, 228, 249: © Lange Uhren GmbH

p. 242: © GettyImages / Luca Ghidoni, FilmMagic

p. 245: Photo 2000 © Cartier

p. 247: © Vacheron Constantin

p. 250: © De Bethune

p. 267: © Jaquet Droz

MARA CAPPELLETTI

A native of Milan, Mara Cappelletti graduated in foreign languages and literature from IULM University, Milan. She then studied the history of jewellery and the history of Eastern art at Sotheby's Institute of Art in London.

A freelance journalist, she is the author of several publications on the history of jewellery, ethnic jewellery and the *Maestri del tempo* ("Masters of Time") series published by 24 Ore Cultura as well as the *Investing in Wristwatches* book series, created in collaboration with Sotheby's and published by ACC Art Books.

Cappelletti designs and curates exhibitions on the themes of jewellery and fashion, as well as conducting research for their catalogues. Among these exhibitions was *Gioielli di Gusto e Stile Milano – Storie di Eleganza* (Milan's Tasteful and Stylish Jewellery – Stories of Elegance), held in February 2020 at Palazzo Morando – Milan's Museum of Costume, Fashion and Image.

She is president of the Associazione Culturale Stile e Storia, which deals with research and appreciation of historical heritage, highlighting the relationship between art, fashion and jewelry as part of the custom of their time.

Since 2019, she has been an adjunct professor in the history of jewellery at the University of Milan as part of the degree course in history and documentation of fashion. Since 2020, she has been collaborating with the Raffles Milan Fashion and Design Institute, teaching the history of jewellery.

Cappelletti also holds conferences and workshops at museums, cultural associations and art galleries.